Christmas in the Heartland

Copyright © 2023 by Daniel Hughes

First printing October 2023

Library of Congress Cataloging-in-Publication Data

Hughes, Daniel
christmas in the heartland / by daniel hughes

 Paperback ISBN: 9798866155132
 Hardcover ISBN: 9798866155569

Published by AR PRESS, an American Real Publishing Company
Roger L. Brooks, Publisher
roger@incubatemedia.us
americanrealpublishing.com

Edited by: Donna Clayton and Amy Brown Thorton
Interior design by Eva Myrick, MSCP

Printed in the U.S.A.

Christmas
in the
Heartland

DAN HUGHES

Table of Contents

Prologue

Reindeer Poop, Wonder Bread Bags, and Rubber Boots

Each year my mother would make a green construction paper advent calendar in the shape of a Christmas tree. The calendar was held in place with magnets on the front of the refrigerator. I did not realize it at the time but each Christmas season it would rise on the door having been moved by mom for age and height.

I am the youngest of five and at my age it still rings strangely in my ears to be referred to as the baby of the family but, labels in the Midwest tend to stick for life. Simple green paper with paper doors hiding a note or message or perhaps a small sketch, was enough to entice a sense of wonderment to one who was young and still believed in the magic of Christmas.

Each night in December right after dinner and I had cleaned my plate Mom would ask if I was ready. I remember hopping in circles in footy pajamas towards the fridge as my mother would point to a numbered door and ask me to read the number aloud before opening it. Often, I would have to try more than once to get it right but when I did, I was rewarded with another surprise hidden behind construction paper. My mother fully understood the power of hope and part of the enchantment of the holidays lies in the anticipation; the thought that something wonderful is just over the horizon and growing closer. When we are children, it is easier to believe. We want to believe. That is the magic of Christmas.

I won't go so far as to say that Christmas is more special in Indiana than anywhere else, but I would like to think so. As we get older, we all tend to cherry pick our memories and at Christmas time our hearts tend to lean towards nostalgia and good thoughts. I don't live in the Midwest anymore and except for occasional visits I have been gone for more than thirty years. Still, a portion of my heart will always reside back home in Indiana. This time of year, perhaps more than others I find myself reflecting on memories. It was my mother's advent calendar which prompted me to write this.

I have been a writer for the last eight years with five completed novels and a motivational book related to my primary career title, but I do not say so as a way of bragging. In fact, no one is more surprised in my passion for words in print than myself. When I was a child, I had a speech impediment so severe it kept me out of kindergarten. Only my family and a few young friends could understand my speech patterns. It was not a mechanical issue for I was provided with the same oratory equipment as anyone else. It was neurological and had to do with the way my brain interprets electrical impulses and the way in which my ears heard things. Added to it, and long before doctors in the mid 1960's had a diagnosis for ADHD (attention deficient hyperactivity disorder,) I was simply labeled as, "A problem child." Our family pediatrician recommended to my parents I be medicated but they refused. ADHD doesn't disappear with age. The symptoms just become less obvious as the one inflicted with it becomes better at masking it in hopes of fitting in and gaining a better understanding of the consequences of one's actions. It is a learning process; but then so is everything else in life.

In my pre-teen years a school counselor also recommended to my parents I should be tested for something called dyslexia. A term I had never heard of but have now lived with my entire adult life. Add it to the list. Later in life in an attempt to find order in a life of chaos I developed tendencies which can only be classified as OCD or obsessive-compulsive disorder. Counting the number of steps between each destination or making sure the pencils on my desk were always in a neat and orderly row. Even numbered, never odd. I am not comfortable with odd numbers. I don't know why. The primary emotions I remember from my childhood begin with nothing less than love and support. The secondary emotion was fear of failing and frustration. I still feel both in near equal quantities but over the years the scales have been tipped in the former more than the latter. For that I am grateful. This time of year, more so than others.

For the last thirty-three years I have worked on national television, yet I would never expect anyone to know who I am, and I am not comfortable with sentences which start with the word,

"I," but it is the easiest way in which to write. My job has been to tell stories of others and the opportunity has offered me more blessings than frankly anyone including myself could have expected. The thought of writing any type of autobiography or memoir always seemed to me to be, well, pretentious. So, please allow me a hall pass. This story is not about the I. It is simply the story of how growing up in the heartland and Indiana Christmas's, along with unconditional love, taught a young boy the most important lessons in life.

My mother's advent calendar was just one of the myriads of tools she used to create excitement as way of teaching me how to count and speak numbers out loud correctly. It was Christmas time, and I was sitting in my office at home working on a separate writing assignment when the memory of construction paper on the fridge came flooding back to me unannounced. It was something I had not thought of in over fifty years. Funny sometimes how it takes so long to learn the important lessons in life and the ones who are the best at teaching them always leave them to be discovered for yourself without hints or a need to take credit for their own wisdom. It turns out my life has been filled with so many examples of such kindness. Will you grant me the opportunity to share those stories with you in hopes that in this holiday season they touch you in the same way they have touched me? It is all I ask. Thank you in advance.

Chapter 1

A Christmas Organ Donor

Family tradition in our home at Christmas time was all about the anticipation. The wait would build excitement. Mom would sit at the ancient pump organ which resided in the family room and play Christmas carols and sing. My father found the organ at an estate sale and took a year and a half to refurbish it in our garage as a present to his lovely wife. My father was an insurance salesman at the time but at his heart he was always an engineer and a craftsman. He knew nothing of the inner workings of a late 1800's pump and reed organ but as he would say, it wasn't hard to figure it out. Seeing literally hundreds of parts and wooden pieces laying on white cloth painters' tarps on the garage floor all labeled with the neat and precise print of my father's hand told me otherwise. I was six years old. I can still hear his most often spoken words echoing in my head, "Danny, if you're going to take on a job do it to the best of your abilities. Take your time and do it right." Turns out he was not the author of those words they were generational. His own father had spoken the same words to him many times.

Both my parents were the product of the Great Depression, and both worked hard to make sure their children had more than they did. We didn't have much, but I don't remember ever being hungry. Fast food was a rare treat for us, "I can make burgers at home," my mother would say. Those words were hers; there was no such thing as fast food in my grandparent's day. For one and a half years my mother was banished from the garage except for the laundry room which was attached to it. My father had simply asked her once not to look under the tarps and knowing my mother she never did. "It's a surprise," he told her, and she knew the value of waiting and anticipation. She had been teaching me the same lesson for years.

Focusing has long been an issue for me and it is not easy to admit one's flaws. I am still easily overwhelmed by tasks I worry are too taxing for my comfort levels. There is an old phrase which goes something like, "Fake it until you make it." When you live in a family who judged honesty as a moral virtue and the measure of one's character I have often felt like a fraud. My father and I are very much different from one another, and I have spent too much time thinking of my own frustrations. It is not easy growing up with a perfectionist but before you judge allow me a disclaimer. It is easy when younger to find anguish in feeling you can't keep up with others. Subconsciously it makes you feel less valued and hopeless. I had heard phrases like, "Pay attention Danny! Or try harder," several times in my early years but those words ended when my father came home with a dilapidated and very worn-out pump organ.

Looking back, I did not know my father worked extra hours and late evenings to pay for a speech therapist for me from the time I was four until age seven. I never gave thought to my mother driving me five evenings a week thirty miles from home and sitting for an hour each time. Children can only think in terms of small circles and few at the time consider the larger orbits which surround them. On an August evening with my mother sequestered to the kitchen it was me my father called out from our crowd of children to come witness it being unloaded from a neighbor's pickup truck. Four of his lodge buddies were offloading what looked less than a musical instrument and more like something which had been dragged on the highway. I couldn't understand my Father's excitement but I was happy he chose to share it with me. "It's for your mother for Christmas Danny!"

"Dad, I know Mom pretty well and I don't think she is going to like it," I told him.

He laughed and said, "You wait. I think she is going to love it once we make it like new again. It's going to take a lot of work though. I could certainly use your help if you're up to it?"

"But ... I don't know how. I...."

He put his hand on my shoulder and said, "Don't worry. I will teach you. Just remember it is for Mom, okay?"

We didn't make the deadline, but he never scolded me, and not once did he make me feel like it was my fault. It took another full year to be completed and I remember sitting on the garage floor on many nights through that first summer and into the autumn and then again, the next year. I sanded spindles, and he showed me how you start with medium or 80 grit sandpaper and then move to 120 and repeat the process with finer and finer grits till the wood was as smooth as glass. He gave me but one task. Mechanical in nature and not over-whelming. Just one. He understood my limitations and yet re-warded me with praise when a simple task had been completed to his uncompromising level of inspection. He did almost all the work himself but never made me feel like an underling. There were many nights when my hand would grow tired, and he would send me to bed to get some sleep and then he would continue for hours, but he never once allowed me to feel like I had failed.

My mother was a musical prodigy. She grew up in Tunkhan-nock, Pennsylvania, which was just another Pennsylvania coal town that had seen better days. There was a kind and elderly neighbor who had an upright piano in her parlor as they called it in that day. My mother, when walking to school, heard her play. At five foot two and red headed she was already a force of nature and knocked on the door and asked the neighbor to teach her to play the piano. She had no money like most people back then but offered to clean out the woman's chicken coups for a chance to learn. My mother was twelve. They studied to-gether for four years. At age sixteen my mother was awarded a partial scholarship to the renowned Juilliard School of Music in New York City. But, partial does not mean complete, and her family did not have the funds to support such a dream. My fa-ther shared that story with me while I sat on a tin bucket in the garage sanding organ spindles, and I am not sure if he was simply reminiscing or wanted me to understand why his gift of an antique pump organ was so important to him. My father, it turns out, was not a perfectionist or task master, as I had once thought. He was just a man who always strived to do things right and one who remembered everything which others cared about. My parents met many years later after she had given up her dream for reality and life's demands. They met during World War II after she had volunteered, and he had been drafted. Well sort of.

He had enlisted in the Marine Corps in the spring of 1942 by choice, two months before his draft number called him up to join the U.S. Army. The Selective Training and Service Act of 1940 required all men between the ages of 21 and 45 to register their name and address for the draft. They then amended the act on December 19th, 1941, twelve days after the Japanese attack at Pearl Harbor, to include registration of any man between the ages of 18 and 64. The most honest man I might ever know lied about his age and had thrown his hat in the ring early. He was only seventeen but with enough high school credits was allowed to graduate early. My Dad left halfway through his junior year of high school. He had already been courted by Purdue University on a potential engineering scholarship. His patriotic duty drove him to enlist. His parents had begged otherwise reminding him his acceptance to Purdue granted him a student deferment; but his mind was made up. His basic training was at Camp Lejeune in Jacksonville North Carolina, (most people would pronounce it like it is spelled or kamp luh zhoon but ask any old school Marine and they will tell you differently. The family of Lieutenant General John Lejeune, whom the base is named for always pronounced their name as if it had an R in it as luh-Jern. So, get it right. Somethings in life are not about textbooks and grammatical protocol and I have learned often times respect outranks the rules.) Afterwards he was transferred a few miles away to Cherry Point Marine Corps Air Station in hopes of becoming a pilot. His draft notice arrived on base, and he was told he had a choice to make. The camp commander told him he could switch his allegiance to the Army Air Corps and with his high school diploma and high-test scores would most likely qualify for officer training and a candidate for flight school. If he chose to stay in the Marine Corps, he would be starting at the bottom and had to work his way up.

"Sir, All I want is to be a pilot and if the Army Air Corps gets me there faster, it seems like the right choice."

"Well that all depends on what type of pilot you want to be Private Hughes!"

"Sir, I don't know if I understand what you mean, Sir?"

"Do you want to fly box cars or fighter planes? This is the Marine Corps. We're looking for the best. The Army Air Corps fly bombers in the European theater, but the Marine Corps is concentrating our efforts with fighter aircraft in the Pacific. We are not just looking for pilots we are looking for the best! Plus, if you stay here, we pay $15 more a month and I will see that you get a shot at flight school. You decide."

My father chose to stay in The Marine Corps. Fifty years later he admitted to me it was the $15 more a month which sealed the deal. The decision most likely saved his life. He never became a pilot. It turns out his partial night blindness was enough to exempt him from pilot training, so he became a tail gunner in a Douglas SBD Dauntless Dive Bomber. He was stationed at Mid-Way Island and saw action in many of the air and sea battles of the Pacific. Had he joined the Army Air Corps he would most likely have become a ball turret gunner over

Germany with a life expectancy of just five missions. The cramped quarters of a ball turret in a B-17 or B-24 where such gunners did not even have room enough to wear parachutes. Plus, if he had chosen The Army Air Corps, he would not have ever met my mother.

I sanded antique mahogany on that garage floor with an intensity and concentration which had escaped me in most endeavors beforehand. An occasional, "How's it going, Son? Looking good. Or, nice Job," were the words spoken by my father to punctuate the other long moments of silence as he worked on harder tasks. It was as much the silence while working together as it was just time spent, I enjoyed most in retrospect. He did not stand over my shoulder judging my work. Instead, he silently allowed me to evaluate my own efforts as to whether or not it was my best or if I could do better. A valuable lesson indeed. At first, I was only hoping to please him. I peppered him often with questions of, "How is this, or is this okay," until I no longer felt the need to question myself on my sanding skills. I know it sounds silly since it was such as simple task but it built confidence. As much as sometimes my little hands hurt, I looked forward to coming home from another frustrating day at school to sit on either the concrete floor or a tin bucket to be with him. His praise of, "Danny that's nice work, well done." kept me going.

My father was meticulous, yet patient. Not just with the pump organ but with me as well, and when it rose once again from parts scattered on the concrete floor of an Indiana garage in December of 1968 to its original glory it was the first time in my life, I felt pride instead of failure. He allowed me the honor of screwing in the newly polished brass plaque just below the keyboard which listed the manufacturer, (Etsy Organ Company, Brattleboro Vermont,) and the date of its original manufacture 1890. 1890, that date seemed like a million years away from my then eight-year-old existence. Now that I am in my sixties a seventy-eight-year-old organ doesn't sound so old, but time is always relative to a child. When you are young time is calibrated in minutes or weeks, not years or decades. It takes a few dozen birthdays and perhaps a few more trips around the sun to bring it all into perspective.

There was just one more task to complete my father's Christmas wish and it was one he admitted he could not do on his own. He was not a musician and had no idea how to tune a seventy-eight-year-old pump organ. My father had rebuilt the bellows which were pumped with both feet allowing air to flow over eighty-eight thin pieces of metal in a frame which corresponded to each of the eighty-eight keys. The pieces of metal are called reeds. There was also something called F stops or draw knobs which are the wooden things you had to pull out to control the air flow on each reed for volume and tone. After reassembling all our work, he sat down and tried it, but each key sounded like someone stepping on a cat.

He somehow found a man who lived in neighboring Illinois who did this type of work in his retirement and my father convinced him to make the four-hour drive to Indianapolis and back on the day before Christmas Eve. If I had thought the organ was old seeing this guy redefined the word old to me. He was in his early 80's and had a hearing aid in both ears. I remember seeing my father scratch his head when the man who introduced himself with, "The name's Cooper Wilson, but you can call me Coop," said hello.

When my father pulled the sheet off the Etsy the man became transfixed. He stared at the organ like it was a long-lost lover and paused several seconds before running his wrinkled hand slowly across the top of the organ I had sanded. "It's beautiful he said. "You never find 'em in this shape. Usually, they are beat to heck and sound even worse." He knew the model number and told us the entire history of the Etsy Company, but my attention span was not the best and the words have been long forgotten. My father showed him polaroid photos of what it looked like at our acquisition and, "Coop," fawned over the restoration. He said the wood working was impeccable. A word I did not know but it was my father's words which made me beam. It was my father who had stained every piece twice and then lacquered each one with long purposeful strokes of a brush remembering he was doing the work for his bride. I had helped somewhat on applying bees wax with one of dad's old undershirts in swirls and circles to bring out the grain, but he had labored for hours to bring the project to its conclusion.

"It's all in the sanding, he told Mr. Wilson. Taking your time, doing it right. Running your fingers over each inch of the wood with your eyes closed until you can feel every bump, ridge, or crack. Then sanding it again until you feel nothing but perfection. Sometimes your eyes miss something, but you can feel when you have done it right." Mr. Wilson nodded already knowing the value of hard work.

I still often close my eyes when I need to concentrate. It blocks out the rest of the world and helps me to focus. What I didn't know was in those moments of silence while working on the garage floor my father's focus was often on me while I worked. My eyes closed with my tongue out just a bit while sanding and feeling the grain of the wood. At first it was in hope I would not disappoint him, but it became more than that. It was a lesson learned to not rush something to just get it done. The magic is never in just the completion of an endeavor it is the satisfaction of staying with it without compromise until each step of the journey fulfills you and you know you have done your best. Looking back, I now know he didn't need my help to accomplish his goal of surprising my mother that Christmas. In fact, I understand he could have accomplished it must faster on his own and taken all the credit, but he didn't.

"Coop, run your hand across the top there again. It feels like marble! It's all in the preparation. Meet the best little sander in the tri-state area," and he pointed at me.

Chapter 2

Organ Recital, Part Two

Looking back now there are three things I remember most about the old man who asked he be called "Coop." The first is he liked to talk while he worked. He lived in Nashville. No, not that Nashville. Nashville Illinois. We tend to think people are different simply because of imaginary lines drawn on maps but I have found it much to be the opposite. But hometown pride is not a bad thing. There are twelve Nashville's in America. Indiana has one as does Arkansas, Georgia, and Kansas. I never understood why so many people look for ways to divide ourselves with differences instead of those things we have in common. When he first stepped out of his well patinaed work truck somehow it caught my eye. It was something about the huge front fenders and rounded hood which stood out as something I had never seen before. Sure, I had seen pick-up trucks before having grown up in Indiana but not like his.

I remember saying, "Wow, cool mister. I like your truck." It would be the second thing about him I most remembered.

"This old thing, he said. It gets me where I need to go. Did I find the right place?" They were the first words spoken in our driveway that day even before he had introduced himself or my father had said hello. "She's a 1952 International Harvester A-110. The 'ole gal might not be too pretty anymore, but she has never let me down." For the life of me I can't tell you why him telling me about such stuck in my brain, but it did. Numbers and letters have long been the bane of my existence, but I repeated his words in my head over and over somehow thinking they were important. 1952 International Harvester A-110.

My father made his introduction and led Mr. Wilson, as I referred to him, towards our garage. I knew the more casual offer of the designation of Coop was never meant towards me. Children back then were expected to be seen and not heard and I knew my lane. I immediately found him to be fascinating. I should have mentioned this earlier, but he looked like Santa Claus. He wore denim overalls and a checkered flannel shirt without a coat in an Indianapolis December. His full beard was white, and his waistline had most likely seen smaller circumferences in his long and storied past. His face was kind and wise. I was always taught not to judge a book by its cover, but you can often judge a man by the lines on his face. If you had grown up where I did, you would understand. I knew he was a farmer even at age eight. I could read the deeply weathered lines on his face. His red cheeks came not from jolliness but from years of sun and wind burn which only come from working outside long before dawn and late into the evening. The dividing line between 1960's suburbia and farmland in Indiana was just across the road or just down the street. The small plot of land on which the house I grew up in was built on what had been farmland just a few years before. Another farmer who's name I do not know who had tired of the struggle and cashed in his chips to a real estate developer with bigger plans. I'm sure looking back; the farmer got a check much larger than what the land had been producing but I wonder if he mourned the decision to have done so for many years later. A hundred years ago 40 percent of American's lived on farms and 60 percent lived in rural areas. Today less than one percent live on farms. Farmers were my neighbors. Sons and daughters of farmers were my school mates. I was right in my early assessment.

Cooper Wilson was a farmer. Dairy. A hundred and eighty head. His son now ran the farm, but he kept his hands dirty. Once a man knows the smell of the Earth and the value of hard work you don't really retire you just slow down a bit. In our first twenty minutes of meeting the man we knew he had lost his wife Margaret ten years earlier and he had one son and three grandchildren. He had played the organ at his local church for more than fifty years and taught himself how to tune. In his later years he had become very much in demand to travel and tune pipe and pump organs. He said without bragging he had once even been asked to tune the organ at Boardwalk Hall in Atlantic City, NJ, the largest pipe organ in the world. "Let's see what you got," he had said, and the story began.

The third thing I most remember about him and the one I purposefully left for last was his flatulence. I know, that was unexpected, but not so much to you as it was to me at my age. When the man who insisted we call him, "Coop," would bend over to get to the inner workings of the Etsy, a small sound would escape from his posterior. Long before I knew the words flatulence or posterior or any comprehension of how to spell either, I knew what a fart was. Ask any eight-year-old boy whether it be in the Midwest or otherwise if a fart is funny and the answer is always yes. Now, I was raised to be respectful and to laugh out loud would have been the opposite but the first one made my eyes grow wide and all I could do was look up at my father with a sense of surprise. My father's stern stare told me to keep it together and my mouth shut. Mr. Wilson's quiet comment of, "Oops, sorry," didn't make it any easier.

Somehow even at that age I knew my father was counting on Mr. Wilson's expertise to see his Christmas vision completed for my mom. The one thing in my life I remember my father could not do was tune an antique organ. So, I bit my tongue. The next note heard was not from the old organ it was once again from Mr. Wilson. His accompanying phrase of, "My fault. Didn't mean to," was enough to fracture me in spasms of silent laughter like a hyena without vocal cords. Seeing my father turn his back to hide his own laughter was almost more than every-thing I had ever been taught about decorum would allow. The old man went back to tinkering with his head deep inside the organ as I did my best to hold it together.

It wasn't easy. There is an old cliché of laughing until you hurt but I can assure you there is something even more painful. It is the feeling of needing to laugh yet not allowing yourself to do so. I suffered the stomach cramps with silent tears in my eyes as a well-behaved son should do, unable to look at any-thing other than the cement floor of the garage. Eye contact of any kind would have tossed me over the abyss. Three deep breaths later I had gathered myself up thinking I had weathered the storm without disappointing my father. I made the mistake of thinking for a split second I had somehow matured in that moment. I was wrong. Fifteen minutes later it was Mr. Wilson who pushed me over the edge.

It was not my fault. I had stood more patiently then any eight-year-old could have ever been asked. The garage was cold that day and I had been standing for over two hours while watching a master craftsman tune an antique organ while sometimes resting his ear with a hearing aid on the mahogany just above the keyboard. Old man "Coop" let out an extended toot which started as a base note echoing with a rumble off the concrete floor and hung in the air with bravado and staccato ending with a high note much like a trombone player drawing the slide closed. I am not sure, but I think it might have been a high "C". The man played a complete octave with his backside. At first, I was impressed at hearing talent beyond my comprehension. After hearing two quick recitals of his true talent earlier I was no longer surprised but never did I expect to witness a virtuoso performance of a musical impresario in our garage. Thinking back, I should have applauded. I should have yelled, "Bravo," as if from the balcony of an opera hall but those are only thoughts in hindsight. Instead, I stood frozen with my cheeks puffed out holding breath behind his back waiting for my father's reaction. I had twice been silently rebuked for almost laughing out loud. My father had taken an unconscious step backwards unresponsive, as if having been pushed by an unseen force of nature. I wanted to laugh. Oh, I needed to laugh but his face read nothing as to how to respond. There were long silences in the garage that day and any child who grew up in the Midwest understands the rules of childhood when dealing with adults. Follow their lead and don't stand out in the crowd. Most importantly never embarrass your parents with unbecoming behavior.

When Mr. Wilson up righted himself, turned and looked at my father and said, "Ooh Sorry.... That was unexpected! Wow, surprised even me!" I lost it. I was done. Crushed. My sides were bursting, and something had to give. I exploded in laughter. The type of laugher which consumes you from within and crumples you to the ground against all will. I looked at my father who was now doubled over from the knees with him still trying to hold himself accountable. When old man Wilson, or "Coop," as I will always remember him, turned first to my father then at me laying on the garage floor he said, "I'm sorry Mr. Hughes, ... I think I might a just killed your boy." My father's knees buckled, and he succumbed to the same level of laughter and tears as my own. I had never seen my dad laugh so hard. Old man Wilson then tucked his thumbs inside the straps of his overalls and looked at both of us; me on the floor and my father barely standing and said, "My fault. I had cabbage for lunch. I should have thought better." With that stoic comment and a small wry smile from a wonderful stranger my father was forced to kneel as if in prayer. Long after the laughter had subsided, my father was still wiping tears from his eyes. Much like my own. In every grown man there is still the heart of a child and in that moment the roles of father and son disappeared for just a bit, and we simply enjoyed life as equals. I have never again laughed that hard or long in my life and I have been blessed to have laughed a lot since then, but nothing like on that day of December 23rd, 1968.

My father had requested my mother run errands and grocery shopping for a while in hopes of keeping his Christmas surprise a surprise. She must have seen the progression of painter's tarps laid out on the garage floor for a year and a half to become the same paint-stained tarps rising to cover what most certainly looked like a piano. Yet she never broke the spell. I never heard her attempt any guesses or ask any questions of what might have resided under those tarps. In complete silence she understood how happy my father was in the project and it was his greatest joy to make her smile. I am sure she was curious, but she was wise enough to understand there is often a greater joy in giving then receiving and she would never wish to diminish such a thought. When Mr. Wilson arrived, I remember her knocking from the inside of the door which separated our kitchen from the garage asking," May I come out now?"

She departed our home after Mr. Wilson and my father had quickly re-draped the Etsy after his earlier inspection with my father throwing a glance towards the old man.

"What do you think" my father asked?

"Give me three hours," he said. My mother understood and left the garage by kissing her palm and blowing it towards my father. I will never understand what old Mr. Wilson did within the bowels of that organ with antique tools and two hearing aids, but what I do remember is him sitting down when he was done and playing. Our garage was transformed into a concert hall, a cathedral and then an old smokey jazz room with rag time songs played with gusto. He finished with a rousing round of, "Take Me Out to the Ball Game," which every eight-year-old boy in Indiana knew back then. I sang along with both of them at the top of my lungs knowing the words. He then sat back well pleased and satisfied in his work and lowered the mahogany cover which made the antique ivory keys disappear from view. He took the time to swipe his hand from right to left slowly as if he was still playing the keyboard. "She's a beauty" he told us. "This has been my pleasure."

My father insisted several times but the man who had asked to be called Coop refused payment. With a few phone calls to neighbors on the one wall phone we had in the kitchen we lifted and carried the organ into the corner of our living room before Mom got home. Coop not only helped; he carried more than his own weight. Christmas came early that year. It was the day before Christmas Eve way back in 1968 but I will never forget it. When my father pulled those same old stained tarps as an unveiling my mother clasped both hands to her cheeks, she reacted with surprise more so for him then for herself. With a huge hug and a kiss, she sat down and played. She played for hours on that evening. She played from memories and dreams she had long thought were long gone. As I think back now, I have tears in my eyes again as I write. Mr. Wilson,

"Coop," drove a long way back to Illinois to be with his own family on that cold December evening with miles ahead of him to return back home. I think he was smiling but I do not know. Knowing folks around here I suspect I am correct. We never saw the old man again but much like spying children hoping to get a glimpse of Santa just once at Christmas time I mentioned to dad the resemblance. My dad still had the forty dollars in his hand he was willing to pay, and he looked at it and put it in his pocket and said, "Maybe he is son, maybe he is." Dad's comment was enough for a memory never to be forgotten.

The organ is still in our family and now sits in my sister Diane's living room. My mother passed just after my twenty-first birthday from lung cancer but at Christmas time I can still smell her Avon perfume which smelled of roses, her favorite, and hear her sweet voice at the organ. As I think back now, I can still feel my father's strong arm around my shoulder as he stood transfixed watching my mother play with a smile on his lips. I did not quite understand until much later in life after I too had fallen in love and married the woman of my dreams. At the time of this writing, we have been married for over twenty years. An eight-year-old boy sitting on a tin bucket in a cold garage in Indiana had been taught one of the most important lessons in life. I saw in his face that my mother's happiness was the greatest source of his own. I will never forget it. He looked down at me and patted my shoulder gently letting me know we were a team, and he was appreciative. I was thankful he had allowed me to be a part of it. It was my greatest Christmas to date.

Chapter 3

The Smallest of Gifts Can Make the Biggest Impressions

That same year my older sister and the first of five kids in our family came home for the holidays unannounced. She is almost fourteen years older than me, and I will admit now I did not know her well. I had not seen her in a couple of years. She had moved away when I was young and the relationship between my sister Janet and my father had often been turbulent. He was a World War II veteran and she a very vocal protester of the war in Vietnam. My father was not comfortable with all the changes which came quickly in the late 1960's. Dirty barefoot men with bellbottom jeans and long hair below their collars. Outspoken women and social unrest. The younger generation had a mistrust for anyone over the age of thirty back then, but it had been the older generation who had sacrificed the most and paid far more than just the bills to provide a better future for their families. The term generation gap was coined in my youth. Opposing theories between fathers and sons, mothers, and daughters on everything from moral values and music to politics and social issues created strife within families but also brought about much needed change. This may sound ridiculous to a younger generation, but I remember my father coming home from work and taking off his tie only to replace it with a thinner tie before coming down to a dinner my mother had prepared. That was his generation.

It was the same Christmas which was filled with so much music and so many smiles on the night before Christmas Eve. When she rang our front doorbell, it was my father who answered its call. When he opened it, he turned and left the door open as he went without speaking back to the kitchen and his cup of coffee. Eight-year-olds are always curious and I was the first to the door as usual, but it was not my place to open it. No one comes calling for anyone my age at nine PM. Plus I had been taught never to open the door to strangers when Mom or Dad were not home. I knew my place in the hierarchy and reaching for the door in front of either when they were in the house would have been a misstep.

So, I stood there. It was mom who had come from the kitchen and welcomed her in with open arms. My father went to bed early without saying much and Janet sat on the couch my parents had purchased from Sears and Roebuck many years earlier with plaid upholstery and the wooden arm rests regaling us with stories of her trip to far away California. She had traveled, "To find herself," she had said but it never made sense to me. We are who we are no matter where we are. Perhaps the extravagance of her Christmas gifts were an attempt to buy favor, yet I don't think so now when looking back.

She left without passing out her presents with my mom saying to her, "It's Christmas eve, let's save those until tomorrow morning. You will be here tomorrow morning, won't you?"

"I didn't know if I would be welcome."

"Janet you're still family. Of course, you are welcome. Give him some time. I will talk to him."

"Good luck with that, I have tried."

"We will talk about it tomorrow. Where are you staying?"

My oldest sister said her goodnight with a hug to each one of us and disappeared as was her usual. She had spent the night at the home of a high school friend. With all the excitement of the holidays and the joy of Mom's Christmas organ I had almost forgotten a partial stranger, yet family, had been there. My thoughts on Christmas Eve were on Santa and reindeer, sleigh bells and sugar plums. By the way I still have no idea what the heck a sugar plum is, but it doesn't matter. I was always the first to awake on Christmas morning even after forcing my tired eyes to stay awake in hopes of hearing hooves on the roof. I am sure it was my mother who installed a family tradition on Christmas morning which allowed my parents to sleep in just a bit more. The opening of their bedroom door was a signal the day could begin but not before. Nothing less than a house fire was cause enough to knock on their door before they made the decision to rise. Instead, it was my second oldest sister Nancy's responsibility when woken usually by me to go downstairs and gather up the stockings we had all hung on the mantel piece the night before and bring them upstairs as quietly as possible.

Nancy would only wake my parents when all four of us had gone through our stockings. We always found an apple or an orange in the toe which never appealed to me. I never thought it was a good idea to eat fruit from a sock. No one ever washes a felt Christmas stocking no matter how many years they had them. There might be a small toy or two or a wrapped candy to enjoy and my mother was always smart enough to know there would be a comic book in mine. I struggled with reading, and it always bought them some more time and rest.

At 8:00 AM my parents' bedroom door would open with a flurry with my father saying, "Who is ready for Christmas," and we were allowed to scamper down the steps to the family room. The tree was lit as usual on Christmas morning, (It was Nancy's responsibility to plug it in before carrying the stockings upstairs.) Santa never showed up before late at night on Christmas Eve. It was Santa who trimmed the tree when I was little and laid out what few presents there were. We always had lights on the outside of the house but few decorations inside until they would surprise us with festivity on Christmas morning. It must have taken my parents many late hours to accomplish, and they must have needed the extra hour or so of sleep. My parents showed their brilliance to me many times. I was just too young to see it.

Janet came through the front door at exactly 10:00 AM. She was always good at making an entrance. I don't think it was her being dramatic. I think it was more her way of simply showing she had done well after moving out so young. Perhaps a message to dad that she too had tenacity and drive. She had bags of gifts. It took all four of the younger siblings two trips to her car to retrieve them. Our second Christmas that morning was much larger than the first or any I had ever experienced. When you are young it is easy to become fixated on wrapping paper and gifts. It takes a bit longer to come to embrace the bigger meaning. I was only eight at the time and wasn't looking for esoteric messages and deeper thoughts. I admit back then it was about seeing what was hiding behind the shiny paper and bows. She had brought dozens of packages. I said dozens as in plural and with dyslexia multiples of any number was hard to comprehend. There might have only been twelve packages under the tree earlier in the morning, but it seemed like a lot. Anything more than one or two for each of us was unexpected.

There was no reason for my sister to try to impress me. In fact, there are few reasons in life to attempt to impress any eight-year-old at all. Eight-year old's seldom have the power to change the course of events in any situation. I don't think she knew it at the time but inspiring a young boy at my age does make a difference and one which can continue to ripple throughout their lives. Kindness at Christmas is like a small stone thrown into a pond. The splash may be small but the circles on the water expand exponentially touching more people than expected. I didn't expect it. She had bags of presents and I do not blame her for enjoying pulling each one out of those bags and handing them to each of us. The first with my name on it was small. The size of a package given makes no difference when it was an unexpected surprise. Are you old enough to remember Match Box cars or Hot Wheels?

Match Box Cars were $1/64^{th}$ scale die cast vehicles manufactured in England by The Lesney Products Company. Their first business venture was a scaled down model of Queen Elizabeth's coronation carriage selling over a million units in The

U.K. in 1953. Since then, they had manufactured small versions of everyday cars and construction equipment like steam rollers, cement mixers and dump trucks. Hot wheels by Mattel here in America on the other hand made shiny brightly colored fantasy vehicles with fast wheels and orange plastic racetracks to play and race with. Mattel launched their die cast in the summer of '68 and they were new to me that Christmas. I had never seen them before. I had a few older Matchbox's which I played with in the dirt by our driveway and by that Christmas they were well worn and well used. The steady stream of small boxes with my name on them continued coming out of that bag like a magician pulling silk scarves from his sleeve. There were fifty all told. Fifty! Match Box Cars and Hot wheels cost 59 cents apiece back in the day, but I felt wealthier than I had ever felt before or perhaps since. I fell in love with vehicles on that Christmas morning.

Later in life I would find magic in the way gears meshed with absolute probability and trustworthiness. I had little faith in my abilities with words or numbers but with patience and preparation gears never lied to me. Those lessons came much later in life but my lifelong love affair with classic cars and vehicles was founded on that day. The first one I opened was a 1955 Chevy 3100 Panel Truck. I had never seen one before, but I thought it was beautiful. It's lines and stance seemed tantalizing and sleek. In fact, though in 1955 it was considered utilitarian and was not designed for automotive fashion. It was the type of truck a plumber might drive; but, to me it was art. I vowed one day I would own the real thing and I did. I found it in a salvage yard in Philadelphia some forty years later just moments before it was to be harshly shoved into a car crusher with a forklift. Long outdated and no longer thought to be of any value other than scrap metal. To me it has always meant much more. I overpaid for it, but it is hard to negotiate when you are emotional and the man driving the forklift knows it from the story he was told. It is still in my collection and working on being fully restored in my limited free time. Patience, and preparation.

I don't remember the order of what toy came out of the bag second or twelfth or forty ninth, but I do remember the third. "That is a 1952 International Harvester A-110 pickup!" I had spoken the words out loud and was talking more to myself than anyone else. Back then I was not known for long sentences. Now please remember any words with more than two syllables were taxing for me. Numbers, especially timelines I still struggle with, but I spoke with complete confidence because I knew the answer. It wasn't a question anyone had even asked but it felt so good to know I was correct before I spoke out loud. I remember my parents' stunned reaction but did not know why.

"Dad, its "Coop's" truck, Dad," and I handed it to him for his inspection and verification. "1952 International Harvester A-110 pickup!" My father knew Lesney printed the year and make of each vehicle on the bottom of the toy, and he looked at it and smiled. He then passed it to my mother who was sitting next to him on the couch and pointed out the letters. The one I handed to him was shiny and blue not olive green and patinaed with rust, but it was indeed the same truck.

It was my mother who seemed most impressed. "How did you know that Danny," she asked. "I don't know. I just remembered for some reason."

"If you can remember that it means you can remember a lot of other things too. We just need to practice…"

I must have driven my mother nuts for months and months after Christmas asking her to quiz me. She had once again found a learning aid outside of textbooks and school exams which motivated me. She would read the bottom of each toy car and I would recite them over and over again. I memorized all fifty cars, and she would sit on the family room floor for hours as I vocalized big words like Lamborghini and Ferrari from memory and lengthy model numbers as well. It was the first time I realized letters, words, and numbers actually had an attachment to those things I enjoyed and not just paper pages and ink. In my 30 plus years on national television I have been blessed to indulge myself in my passion for vehicles which started on that day. I have owned over a hundred vehicles in the past four decades and few have been the truly expensive exotics but there have been a few.

Seven years ago, I partnered with a friend to rent commercial space and open a classic car restoration shop and ran the business without salary or income in hopes of building a sideline business and helping others with a passion for vehicles to achieve their goals. I enjoyed the comradery of working with craftsmen and mechanics, but it was never financially viable and Covid brought the business to a close as it did many others. I closed the doors in January of 2021 at a substantial personal loss financially, but I have no regrets. I had been paying my employees' salaries out of pocket for months on end and even sold cars in my private collection to keep the business afloat. During those tough times there was still food on the table for those who I employed and worked with me, and I still think of myself as having been blessed for being able to do so. My business partner was smart enough to know in the second year the chances of success were limited and asked me to buy him out to limit his current loses so I did. Two years later he also showed me how buying the property would be a good idea and we once again became partners but now in real estate. He is older than me and always wiser and my appreciation for his mentorship speaks no limits.

When it became apparent it was time to say enough, I closed the shop sadly but was able to rent out the shop space for profitable revenue and was able to retain the warehouse on site to house what is left of my collection. Those people who were next to me on the day I shut those doors were not just prior employees the day before they were family and always will be. No one was surprised and all had months to prepare for future work but there was still a sinking feeling I had let them down. I was touched when none admonished me for my failure and even more so surprised with their compassion towards me in knowing a dream had not worked out. Knowing all of them have gone on to prosper with future endeavors I was not able to provide makes me happy for them. We are all still close and talk frequently as true friends should do. I made a bad business decision which cost me a lot, but in return I gained people who will be there with me for life. Education is always expensive and not to be evaluated only on a spread sheet with dollars and cents. Most things in life are more important than money.

Thomas Edison failed more than a thousand times before coming up with a viable filament for the electric light bulb. When pressed in an interview with American Magazine in 1921 he was asked how it felt to fail so many times. His response was epic. "I didn't fail. I found a thousand ways it didn't work."

Even with my sister Janet's extravagance it might have been just one of those tiny toy cars which sparked my passion. Even the smallest of gifts given in kindness can inspire. She had several packages for each one of us. My mother, older brother and three sisters. She saved the last for my father. One gift, not many, just one. I only remember it to be a small wooden box. It wasn't wrapped or dressed up with a bow to impress. She pulled it from the bottom of all those bags and quietly said, "Dad, this is for you. I would prefer you open it in private if you don't mind." Both got up and walked into our kitchen and I remember my father opening the box and staring at its contents for a long time without speaking. It was meant to be a private moment but all of us in the family room were looking, of course. I may never know what was in that box and it is not my place to ask even if curious after all those years. Moments such as those are special and not to be shared. He looked up and paused and then hugged her. I had not seen him gather her in his embrace like that in many years and it was my mother who understood it was their time and not ours and directed our attention back to her new, yet antique organ and once again began to play.

Chapter 4

Presents for Santa

I am sixty-two years old and in all the Christmases I remember, and believe me my memory is strong, I simply cannot conjure up an image of any one particular gift Santa ever left for me under the tree. You were told with the one exception of the year with many toy cars we never had a lot of gifts and I said so without any complaints. It was midwestern suburbia circa 1969. Almost everyone we knew had similar financial circumstances and children don't judge other children by income level unless taught to do so by parents. Adults it seems are much more concerned about such things. We had a nice two-story house identical to all the others on our street with exception of different colored shutters and perhaps front doors. My older brother and I shared a bedroom as did two of my sisters who were still living at home. There was always food on the table, and we all had our two sets of clothes; those for school and those for play and God help the child who confused the two. Each of us got a new winter coat each year even if it meant a hand me down from an older sibling, still it was new to us that year. No one was out to impress anyone. Things were just what they were, and it was fine.

Christmas back then was not as commercialized. There was a purity and an innocence about the holiday. Hot chocolate with mini marshmallows was reason enough for joy. I don't know which statement is truer: I adore Christmas or is it that I adore what this time of year represents. A time of year when people try to be their best. Kinder, more hopeful. Generous with a spirit of giving for the sake of the smile you create on someone else's face is more than enough to feel happiness without thinking of what you might receive in return.

When I was little, I found it sad the one who gave so much got so little in return. A plate of cookies and perhaps a glass of room temperature milk seemed like less than the man in the red suit deserved. Santa was way cooler to me way past the time most of my friends still believed. I wanted to meet him. The real him. Not the fake one dressed up in a cheap felt costume at the mall. Kids are not stupid even those of us with cognitive challenges and never discount the thought process of a child. I knew there must be at least thirty different malls in this country, maybe even more if that were possible, and Santa can't be at all of them at the same time to greet children for photo ops and toy requests. I figured it out on my own early on. Those false Santa's were decoys, plants, spies if you will and all working for the big man while passing information back to him while too busy at the North Pole in December to leave his post. Any child under the age of ten is fully aware of his naughty and nice list. I had seen Christmas specials on TV where Santa had a magic snow globe which allowed him to keep an eye on every child on Earth, but I have always been a realist and never believed in such hocus pocus. Spies just simply made more sense.

I remember smiling at naive toddlers a few years younger than me while standing in line, but I would never think to say so. I forgave them for not being as wise as myself. Sharing the secret simply to impress others with the age-old game of, "I know something you don't," would have broken the spell and the spell itself was part of the magic of Christmas. Plus, I knew what it was like to have people remind me how often they were smarter than myself.

My mother was the smartest person I knew, and I only shared my discovery while sitting on the front bench seat of our Plymouth station wagon on the way home from the mall. I hesitated for a bit but figured out with her intellect she must have come to the same conclusion at least a year or two before me. I posed it as a question though just in case. "You know that wasn't the real Santa, right?"

"Why do you say that Danny?"

I explained my well thought out hypothesis including the mathematical calculations of multiple children at multiple malls and factored in Santa's work ethic and staunch track record of always delivering on time and the ridiculousness of him taking time out during his busy season solely for the purpose of making personal appearances. Sure, the guy was a worldwide celebrity and at my age perhaps the most famous person I could name but he never seemed to be in the game for the limelight. I was never good at math, but I knew the numbers didn't add up plus I knew Santa as if he was a friend and like my father, I figured he was always on task and would not tolerate disappointment.

She paused for a moment while driving and listening and then said while holding her index finger to her lips. "You're right Danny. But that is a secret. You can keep a secret, can't you?"

I nodded my head vehemently knowing we were on the same page and fully considering the consequences of perhaps ruining someone else's Christmas magic. I had already committed to the same mental pinky swear with myself before bringing up the conversation on the way home, but I knew I could tell my mom anything. After her confession I had but one concern. "Do you think Dad knows?"

"I think he figured it out," she said.

Later that evening while helping my mom to dry dishes I had done a lot of thinking about the previous conversation about my own observations and posed a question. "Mom, this year would it be okay to leave a gift for Santa?" I still thought Santa made Matchbox cars and Hot Wheels at the north pole like he did with all toys. I had never thought of where toys really come from. At nine there was no thoughts of global supply chains and manufacturing. No understandings of retail distribution, warehousing, packaging, shipping, marketing, vendor relations or customer support. Much like most adults today, we rarely give much thought to how most any item got onto our store shelves to begin with, but the fact is every single product you ever purchase or consume has a human element behind its creation. It is easy to forget how hard someone must have worked to provide what we have easily grown accustomed to.

It was twenty years later such terms and knowledge became my life's work.

For the record I spent more than half my life as a television host on the world's largest televised shopping channel QVC. My job was to help inventors and entrepreneurs to develop their ideas and then present them to a national television audience and it was always more than just a paycheck to me. The expectations of my youth didn't count for much so being in a position to help others was equally as rewarding as an income. In my thirty-three-year tenure as an employee of QVC I trained over five thousand on air guests. Many of which had never been on TV. In March of 2023 with consumer buying habits changing and stockholder confidence waning I was let go. I wasn't alone. Another dedicated host with nineteen years of service was also fired along with 398 others who worked hard behind the scenes but also found themselves unemployed. We were told it was a simple cost-cutting measure. They fired me over a zoom call. Two months later the company hired four new hosts hoping to replace the revenue stream two hosts with the combined experience of fifty-two years in the industry had consistently produced. I don't pretend to understand the mindset of bean counters in multi-billion-dollar corporations, but I come from simple roots where loyalty and work ethic counted for something.

Currently, there are just over a hundred and fifty people worldwide who do exactly what I did for a living and even fewer who have done it for so long. My job was to help make peoples' dreams come true. Inventors who perhaps have sketched out their product concept on a napkin at their kitchen table and a year later making it available to consumers on a scale few can fathom. When I started there in the summer of '89 few people had even heard of the fledgling start up cable network but today it is a household name and one of the largest retailers on the planet. None of which makes me any type of celebrity and there will always be far more people who know nothing of me then there are who do and I'm okay with that. I am proud of what I've done. The impact of my work has changed many peoples' lives and it is not just selling stuff on TV. At the highest level of any profession there are always pressures. Vendors and manufacturers, individual inventors counting on your assistance to achieve a small slice of the American dream. You deal with it. You overcome it. I am just thankful I was given the chance and earned my way accordingly. I would never have taken a two-dollar bet on my own success back then even if the odds paid out in millions. I bet my mother would have though.

"Mom, what should I give Santa," I asked?

"Well, it all depends on how much you love him. You will do the right thing," and she left the decision to me. Santa got a Hot Wheels car that year. It was still in the blister pack from the year before because I didn't want to damage it or play with it. Hot Wheels had released their first sixteen cars in May of the previous year. The same year my sister Janet gave it to me. Collectors refer to those originals as the redline series due to the red pinstripes on the wheels. It wasn't my favorite though and I look back with a sense of guilt for not having been willing to part with more. I was nine and wasn't prepared to give up the ones I had truly fallen in love with like the 1955 Chevy Panel Truck or Coop's International Harvester pick up, but it was still new, and I thought he would like a new one in the package more than one I had played with.

From May of 1968 to present day the Mattel Corporation has produced more than four billion die-cast cars. It was model number 6205 Custom Camaro in metal flake blue paint. It was shiny and looked fast and I thought he would like something other than a red sled with some real horses under the hood instead of just eight reindeer.

The next year Santa got his usual bribery of home-made sugar cookies but on that Christmas, he also received a baseball autographed by hall of famer and right fielder Roberto Clemente. My father had given me the ball after meeting him when the superstar had been hired as a keynote speaker at an insurance convention my father attended earlier, before spring training. My father thought I would like it since I too played right field in my local little league. I was no Roberto Clemente. Little League in Indiana was a time-honored rite of passage to a pre-teen boy in the Midwest, and kids my age were signed up regardless of athletic ability. I picked a lot of dandelions out there in right field behind the elementary school I attended during those days. Plus, Roberto Clemente played for the Pittsburg Pirates for eighteen years and I was a Cincinnati Reds fan since they were the closest pro team to my hometown of Indianapolis. I knew every player on Cincinnati's starting lineup but had not heard of Roberto Clemente. So, at Christmas time I asked Dad if it was okay to give it away and he said yes.

Two years later in December of 1972 Roberto Clemente lost his life in an airplane crash while on a humanitarian mission to provide supplies to earthquake victims in Nicaragua. The hall of fame waved their rule of induction into their coveted fraternity of having to wait five years after retirement before being accepted into their ranks due to his stellar career and his generous charitable works. Pittsburg retired his number and The MLB, or major league baseball, renamed its annual Commissioner's Award in his honor. Less than one percent of all major league players will every make it to the hall of fame. Earning the distinction of being named the Roberto Clemente award recipient says much more about the individual then just their prowess in playing a simple game. Roberto Clemente became my baseball childhood hero.

I know much more about a great athlete and a great man today then I did back then and my gifts to Santa only lasted those two years. I had become wiser in terms of the world and completely forgot about those gifts until many years later. As usual it was my mother who would remind me of innocence and kindness.

The gifts under our tree given by Santa in my youth were not spectacular. They were needs. Socks, maybe or perhaps underwear but it did not matter. Seeing his name on the to/from tag still created excitement. It was a way of knowing you had made his list as nice instead of naughty. Often times I worried about which list I might be held accountable for. Not by any parental threats although I hear adults doing it at Christmas all the time, ("Eat your broccoli … Santa is watching,") but because my own actions were often taxing to my parents. Because I was dyslexic and ADHD frustration became a primary emotion and when textbooks were a blur and numbers a jumble which were undecipherable, I acted out. My father's tolerance for such was less than my mom's and he would often walk out of the room shaking his head to leave her to deal with the fallout. A present from Santa meant he remembered you and had not forgotten your heart and still felt you were worthy of his kindness, even with the outbursts of frustration and frequent meltdowns.

My parents also understood a bigger picture. One I feel we all might have all forgotten. Adults will always have their office gossip over a cup of coffee at work, but it pales in comparison to the speed of communication of prepubescent children in elementary schools after the holidays. Parents should not use Santa Claus' generosity as a measuring stick for his love and approval. When Mary got a pony, and you received underwear a child starts to wonder. Shouldn't just being included into the circle of love be enough? The first question asked by children after the winter break is always, "What did you get for Christmas," and there will always be someone with more than yourself. That's life in general and children understand it as much as adults. I will never begrudge those with more than myself and I have known too many people in the business world who feel there are only so many dollars out there in the world and if someone else has one of them it's just one less for them to acquire. Those people tend never to be happy. It is the second question of, "And what did Santa bring you," which raises doubts. When Mikey got a bicycle from St. Nick, and you got socks it no longer becomes a question of whose parents might make more money than yours it bears to ask if Santa might care for some more than others. My parents understood the message and did their best to keep the holidays as simple pleasures and not a competition.

I adored my mother. She was my champion and my guardian. She was one who looked past my difficulties but refused to allow them to be excuses. Dad was more pragmatic with kindness, but she was emotional like me. When she passed away, I was destroyed. I was twenty-one but in so many ways my emotional and educational development had been stunted by slow growth and insecurities brought on by prior struggles. I still feel guilt for not being there for my father as much as he had always been there for me during that time. Consumed with my own grief I just assumed as usual he was stronger than me.

Dad called me a few months after the funeral. We had spoken every day over the phone but with work and my first steps at adult life and responsibilities I found myself using a far too common excuse of being busy. I only stopped by a couple of times a week. Mom had passed away in October and Dad asked me to come by unexpectedly. We sat at the kitchen table for a while, and I asked how he was doing. He said it wasn't easy, but he was getting by and then mentioned he had been going through her things and he found something I might like to have. He took me up to the attic which was above our garage. The same one I had sat underneath on a tin bucket sanding mahogany so many years before. There was a pull-down folding ladder accessed with a rope which allowed our entry, and I wasn't surprised to find the attic clean and meticulous like his garage. He always had peg boards above his work benches with painted outlines of tools he had acquired over the years to show if anything had been missing. He had baby jar lids from five kids screwed underneath shelving to hold screws, nuts, and bolts. He always knew if something was gone. It was like inspector Clouseau met This Old House but that is my dad. I had not been in the attic in years. The plywood flooring was painted and cobweb free and he walked me to an old steamer trunk towards the back and opened it.

"She saved this for you," he said. He pulled out a yellowed cardboard box and opened it and handed it to me. Inside was a Hot Wheels car still in the blister pack and a baseball. I had to laugh. I hadn't thought of either in many years. In fact, it took me a second to remember them at all. "Wow, why would mom keep these after all those years," I asked?

He smiled. "She kept everything Dan. Anything to do with you kids." He got up and walked to a different corner of the attic and pointed to several boxes. The type with fake wood printed on the outside and used for storing file folders. There was a box for each one of us kids with our name written on it in her delicate hand. "May I," I asked?

"Sure, it's yours." Inside was every report card I ever received good or bad. Notes from teachers, again good and bad. Certificates from Little League Baseball and any other citation I had ever been awarded up and throughout my high school years. There was a small plaster cast of my palm print I had made in third grade class and painted red for Valentine's Day. I had to smile thinking back as to how I thought it was the dumbest gift ever to give your mother, but teachers are always smarter than kids and she had probably been a mother herself and knew its true value for the future. I couldn't help but put my adult hand over the imprint trying to remember what such little hands felt like. There were also ten different green construction paper advent calendars each marked on the back for the year she had made them. At twenty-one years of age, I really had not felt like I had accomplished much but in my mother's eyes, my eyes were not her own. She kept it all. The box was heavy and full. "Brings back memories doesn't it, son?"

"Yeah, it sure does." We spent over two hours sitting on old chairs in the attic going through things and trading stories. His memory much longer than mine. He told me stories of how they met and the moment he knew he was in love. I reminded him of, "the great fart of 1968," which for some reason he had forgotten. Perhaps it had been surpassed by his joy of seeing Mom so happy with his gift that year. We sat for hours laughing and reminiscing. He tried to apologize for little league games missed while working and other things, but I stopped him. He lightened the mood by punching me on the arm and said, "Do you want to see something funny?"

"It all depends. Is it at my expense?"

"Yes, of course it is," he laughed. He took me back to the first box with the toy gifts I had given Santa. On the underneath side of the top was an envelope taped to it. Inside were the two letters written to Santa. I will only bore you with one but the second was equally as difficult to read:

Deer satna claws.

Mary krismaz. Thank you for the przents you have givn me for so lon. I waned to say thank you and sho you my pre-ciation for being so nis. It not new but I nevr open it and I hop wen you can play it maks you hapy. Daniel A. Hughes

I had signed it in the formal manner as one should do when engaged in such important matters. Looking over my shoulder Dad said, "You really sucked at spelling you know that right?"

I chuckled. "Yes, I fully remember." I also remembered the dictionary in the other box and did not need to have picked it up or open a page to remember ten words a week highlighted in yellow ink for me to memorize. She would pronounce the words over and over and I did the same until they were correct. Then with patience she would help me memorize each one's spelling. Letter by letter. Memorization nothing more. The mental process of word structure and grammatical rules were still beyond my comprehension, but she knew my memory was strong. She always played to my strengths and helped me to develop them.

Sounding out a word is not a practical way in which to learn the English language. Especially when dyslexic. The word "phonetically," is spelled starting with the letters P and H. You would think it would be the one word they spelled starting with an F instead. Our grammatic forefathers had a wicked sense of humor. If you are old enough to remember a teaching aid for adults and children who struggled to read which was advertised on TV called, "Hooked on Phonics," then you might remember the commercials. I doubt though you will remember the telephone number used in the advertisement in which to order the product. I do though. It was 1-800-ABC-DEFG. Great marketing ploy ... but if you struggle with the alphabet and have difficulties in reading it really wasn't much help.

I'm sure some brilliant person in their marketing department was applauded and patted on the back for such creativity but in the early days of touch tone telephones any phone number using letters instead of numbers was simply a pain in the ass. They still are and not just to those of us with learning disabilities. I wonder how much business they lost from people who could not decipher the alphabet in order to actually buy the item advertised to help them. Had it not been my mother and countless hours at the kitchen table I still wonder if today I could spell my own name correctly?

A vintage original 1968 model number 6205 Custom Camaro in metal flake blue and still in the package is extremely rare and collectors would pay thousands of dollars for it. A signed Roberto Clemente ball even more so being valued in the tens of thousands. I only know that because of having them appraised for insurance values but will never part with either for any amount. The memories mean much more. Funny how giving a gift often times has a way of paying you back in more ways than one can expect. Especially when the gift is given with no expectations of a return on the investment of kindness. I hugged my father goodnight that evening and said, "She was a remarkable woman, Dad."

"She still is. She worked hard to teach you Dan even when some of your teachers had given up on you. I'm sure she taught you lessons you are not even aware of yet. They will come to you over time. In some ways she will always be with you. Guiding you. Helping you. Just like she will always be with me," and he pointed to his heart and smiled.

Chapter 5

Kindness Counts as a Gift

I don't like labels. Neither did my parents. I had challenges but Mom and Dad refused to refer to them as disabilities or allow me or anyone else to use them as an excuse. Countless hours of repetition and kindness on behalf of my parents were lessons taught without my knowledge and what they taught me has stuck with me throughout the years. Dad was one who found it difficult to compromise on his own expectations and it carried over to the expectations he had for his children. He demanded his best from himself and expected the same from his children.

My mom always saw what few strengths I had, and I am sure long after I had fallen asleep it was her who spoke of them to my father while behind their closed bedroom door in whispers and hushed tones telling him to be patient. My father always respected my mother's intellect and as hard as he worked to feed five kids, he always heeded her advice.

In sports there is a term referred to as muscle memory. It is the practice of repeating the same physical movement so often it becomes second nature. Pitchers in baseball do it. So do batters. Standing on the mound or at the plate thousands of times until they no longer need to think through a mental process to navigate the mechanics of the physical action with a higher probability of success. My mother was smart enough to ask the question as to whether the process might work in reverse. If one could train muscles to remember with repetition could memory itself be worked as a muscle by using the same process? She had started with little cars on the floor of my family room.

I tend to think in pictures not words. So, my mother made flash cards she had drawn herself. Simple one syllable words where it was not the letters which stood out it was the image first with the letters woven into the picture in such a way as to connect the two together in ways I had never seen. The cat I would see had been drawn where the letter C was making up the curve of its left shoulder. The A was the separation of two front paws and the T the edges of a top hat tilted at a jaunty angle upon the cat's head. I wasn't spelling or sounding out for those ways of learning made little to no sense with my disorder. I was memorizing. Cat: c, a, t. There is an amazing strength in a child's mind when they know they know something. They are no longer guessing or simply hoping to be correct. She made hundreds of those flash cards, and we sat at the kitchen table for hours on end. Those of us who navigate dyslexia find it difficult to make correlations between words. Even today if I were shown a picture of a feline with the written word of kitten beneath my mind will always go directly to the word cat verbally before my eyes can make out those letters.

She did the same with math. It was all memorization and never the actual working of an equation. I could not trust my own eyes. Nines on paper are easily confused for sixes just upside down. Fives look like twos just reversed. Threes and eights are the same when wondering if the one who wrote them just didn't finish the final loops to complete the circles. I had made so many mistakes in my own education I had empathy for others wondering if they might have made a mistake themselves, so I questioned myself in the same situation. Is it a three or did they really mean an eight? The constant thought process is exhausting and there is no greater exasperation then when on a math quiz the teacher asked us to, "show your work."

Hundreds of flash cards and years at the kitchen table with a woman who surpassed any mandates of patience to require saint hood had taught me how to get correct answers, but I was still judged by the way in which I had gotten there. I find that sad. Not for myself, for I had come to be accustomed to being called wrong but for her in knowing how hard she had worked to make me better just to be told the correct answers were not always satisfactory. What seemed to matter back then was a singular pathway taught in a textbook instead of innovation, understanding and love. After having been delayed entry into kindergarten and being held back in second grade I graduated, if you can call it that, from sixth grade with a C average in math. In my last semester of that year more than 90% of my test questions were answered with correct answers but when asked to show my work and the explanation of, "I just know the answers," my test scores were dropped to 50% which is a low D. 49% would have meant failing the subject with an F.

Will you allow me to offer a bit of life advice? Never challenge a five-foot two red headed mom from the Midwest. When my mother saw my last report card she was pissed! That is my word to describe the situation not hers for she never swore. The next day she dragged me into Allisonville Elementary School in Indianapolis by the hand to the principal's office. Thankful she was not angry with me I tagged along not even knowing what her anger was. I had passed. I got a C. To me it meant another school year without repeating a grade. It meant moving on to Junior high school and not being left behind from friends, again. Most importantly knowing I had not failed and my father who was my hero would not be disappointed. As a mother and a champion, she was not satisfied with status quo. "Mr. Selmer, she said. Please call Mrs. Wilson to your office and ask her to bring her math textbook and her final quiz paper!" Mr. Selmer was our principal and a kind man. With my speech impediment earlier in life I had trouble pronouncing his name. Often times children with dyslexia tend to mispronounce words and names by not knowing how to repeat sounds and the oratory practice of learning of where to place your tongue in your mouth in which to recreate the appropriate sound. Another skill learned by repetition and memorization. For years I had referred to him as Mr. Thelmer with a TH instead of the S. I remember countless times in the hallway before classes with him stopping me without aggravation to coach me as he greeted every student in the main hallway as the buses emptied and the school day would begin. He would put his hands on my small shoulders without reproach and repeat his name with a long and an exaggerated S, "Like the word snake. Sssssssnake," he would say. I remember the day in fourth grade I pronounced it correctly after hundreds of attempts and he hugged me. He and my mother were cut of the same cloth I just did not know it at the time.

Lessons taught in textbooks and those lessons taught by life don't always have equal value. Both have an impact but when choosing to teach with only one method children are often left out or left behind.

Mrs. Wilson showed up a bit sheepishly. I had been asked to sit in the outer office, but I could see my mother waving an angry finger in Mrs. Wilson's face through the window. I also saw Mr. Selmer step between the two ladies when Mrs. Wilson said something with her back arched and my mother walked to the door and called me inside. Her tone was calm and loving but I could tell she was mad. "Danny, your teacher has a question for you. Answer her honestly!"

Mrs. Wilson stammered a bit not expecting to have to confront a thirteen-year-old with developmental issues. "You made an accusation Mrs. Wilson why not ask him directly?

"Mrs. Hughes, I know Daniel has, well, struggled with his schoolwork. I know he works hard, and it is why I gave him a passing score."

"Ask him." my mother repeated.

"I, ... I."

"Danny, she wants to know if you cheated on your final exam?"

"No ma'am!"

"How did you come to know those answers," my mother asked?

"Because we practiced them."

"Mrs. Wilson ask him any one of those fifteen questions on the final exam!" Mr. Selmer reached for a piece of paper and a pencil from his desk. "No, Mr. Selmer he is dyslexic, and writing is still difficult for him and takes him much longer. It confounds him and wears down his self-confidence worrying he will put letters and numbers in the wrong order. "Just ask him a question, out loud." Mrs. Wilson did.

It took me a few seconds, but I knew the answer and told her so. "Another," my mom said. Same result. "And another!" I felt good. Both Mrs. Wilson and Mr. Selmer looked a bit surprised. "Part of my responsibility as an educator is to assess a student's knowledge of the learning process itself. It's why we ask them to show their work Mrs. Hughes," Mrs. Wilson said.

"If you wouldn't mind Mrs. Wilson open your textbook to any of the sample test questions in the last six chapters. You told Danny any of those questions would be on the final exam. There are thirty sample questions, but you only used fifteen. Ask him one not on the test." She did and I got it right.

"How?"

"He memorized every one of those questions and then memorized every answer. He practiced writing those answers a hundred times and only missed two because he confused his sixes with his nines. He worked harder in your class than anyone else and still struggled but he did not give up. You asked for correct answers and he gave them. Do you have children?"

"Yes, I do Mrs. Hughes."

"Then you understand. If I want to teach my son not to touch a hot stove, there is more than one way to do so. I can sit back without warning and let him learn the hard way and perhaps it will be a lesson he never repeats but I prefer to protect him from being hurt. I remind him often to be careful. He may never understand the process and thought patterns of your math quiz, but he deserves to have won one battle and feel-good knowing working hard and working within his strengths still breeds confidence. He has been burned too many times by textbooks. I want my boy to head towards Junior High School thinking he can do anything if he puts his mind to it. Even if the work he has to do means more hours than anyone else and even if the work he has to show doesn't fit your curriculum or the way in which you were taught to teach."

(Okay. Those are mostly my words many years later after working more than ten-thousand hours or more on my own vocabulary, but I do remember my mom's reference to our stove. I also remember Mr. Selmer putting his hand on my shoulder once again and saying, "Young man. I am impressed.")

On my last day of sixth grade Mrs. Wilson threw a small party. The schoolwork was done, and she had put up balloons and streamers. We played games and laughed. At the end of the day, she had an awards ceremony and everyone in the class was awarded something. She had printed out certificates of merit and my name was called last. I saw my classmates walk to the front of the class before me and as the number of students became fewer and fewer, I started to feel as I had often felt before. I shrank in my seat and wanted to hide. Disappear. I never wished to be the center of attention but sometimes being the last one to be noticed does just that. When she finally called my name, I walked to the front of the class like a dead man walking. She said, "This is a special award and one I wanted to save for last. This is for you, and I am so proud to present it to you." She read the words in gold leaf and calligraphy which stated for everyone to hear. "To Danny Hughes, most improved student of the year!" She went on to say, "He got a 90% on his final exam. Well done. You earned it!"

I didn't mean to. I didn't want to, but I cried with embarrassment. I had cried in classrooms before and at recess when I stayed inside while others played outside when not fitting in, but this was different. I once had a teacher who scolded me at the chalk board when numbers confounded me and was told to just go sit down. When silent tears erupted, she told the other students to ignore me for I was just looking for attention. That was never the case. I have never sought attention. In fact, I have spent most of my life avoiding it. Still, it often came my way.

When she handed me the certificate students who had made fun of me earlier in the year with comments of stupid or worse applauded. Some of the worst offenders even stood while clapping and I cried even harder. Children can be very mean without knowing the impact of their actions but on that day the impact of those who I thought were my adversaries or even enemies for calling me out for being different from themselves became ones I loved in the moment. Mrs. Wilson took me in her arms and hugged me as if I was one of her own children. Classmates I felt I had never bonded with before patted my shoulders. Tears are tears but just like the pathways to education and self-awareness both often come from different directions and mean different things. In the moment I was uncomfortable being the center of attention, but the tears were not of shame or failure for the first time in my life in public. Never discount the awareness of children. The kindness of my classmates brought additional tears to Mrs. Wilsons eyes as well. For the next few years of my education, I had former classmates and allies who covered my back when moving into Junior High School and new associates. Those who had once bullied me refused to allow others to do the same. To those who watched over me I cannot find a way to say thank you. Some emotions are hard to capture simply with words.

Mrs. Wilson corresponded with my mother by letter each year through out my junior high years and into high school. I wasn't aware of this until years later while going through the box my mother had kept. Those letters made me smile on the night dad and I sat in the attic but meant even more to me several years later. The letters had stopped decades earlier until one day she was in her living room and happened to turn on the TV to the network I proudly represented for over thirty years. She had retired and Mom had passed many years earlier, but the letter addressed to her was still delivered to the old home address and my father opened it. I must have made a reference to having been from Indianapolis during a show and might have even mentioned Allisonville Elementary School. In her letter she stated how I might not even remember her, but she had remembered me. Her kind letter to my mother was tucked inside a Christmas card.

My Father called me and read it aloud. One of the toughest teachers I had ever encountered, and there were many, gushed at having seen me on TV. She used words like proud and accomplishments and expressed a genuine happiness in my success without taking any credit at all for herself in the process. She also included her phone number, and I called her. By circumstance it happened to be on Christmas Eve 1992. I did not call her in hopes of continued praise or retribution for her earlier toughness. It was a call simply to say thank you for the kind letter and card and nothing more. We talked for over an hour.

When you're a child it is hard to think of teachers as human beings like the rest of us. If you saw one at the grocery store and outside of the classroom the juxtaposition of seeing them outside of their element of authority seemed unnatural. As if teachers don't also eat. I can't explain it any better. It is just the way a child thinks. Even as an adult it is often difficult to separate long remembered ranks of authority and child. I kept her number and called her once a year on Christmas Eve to say hello and chat for a bit. By 1996 she was not doing well and in November just before Thanksgiving of that year she passed away. Dad called me the day he read her obituary in The Indianapolis Star newspaper. The funeral was two days later, and I had no days off to fly to Indianapolis and return back to Philadelphia without missing work, and fourth quarter is our busiest time of year. I would have liked to have been there to pay my respects, but being an adult sometimes means making decisions prescribed by the demands we think are part of the paycheck. I thought back to so many missed little league games and had a better understanding of my father and the sacrifices he had made in order to pay the bills and feed five hungry kids. I think he missed not being there for those more than I did not having him present. It takes a while for a child to think of the shoes filled by a parent.

I'm not sure why I did it, but I still had Marie's home phone number and decided to dial it. I knew she was gone, and, in my defense, I only refer to her as Marie at her own insistence from the first call on Christmas Eve 1992. Habits are hard to break when you grew up in the Midwest and were always taught our manners when dealing with those older and wiser. I still say sir and ma'am when addressing people older than myself out of learned politeness. I am sure one day I will be called out for it with the current climate of pronoun offensiveness when intent is no longer considered and being correct is all which matters. Somewhat the opposite of my earlier struggles when showing your work and your efforts to do the right thing seem to count for less than only getting the answer correct by those who currently appoint themselves to be judge.

Marie always referred to me as Danny which as I grew older was a nickname, I did my best to separate myself from. Not that I was ashamed of my past it was just a way of distancing the long ago from who I had become. There will probably most likely always be a part of me who never escapes all childhood insecurities but today most people just call me Dan by casual request. Often times in business meetings when greeted by someone I had not met before they will refer to me as Mr. Hughes and they are always responded to in the same manner. "No, please. That's my dad's name. Just call me Dan. It's nice to meet you."

Marie deserved the hall pass simply out of time and memory. Her phone rang twice, and someone picked up. It was her daughter Laurie. There was a second or so of discomfort before she said hello.

"Hello, I said. "I don't wish to bother you and I truly hope I am not intruding during your time of grief, but I heard of her passing and simply wished to express my condolences."

"Who is this," she asked?

"My name is Dan Hughes, and she was my sixth-grade teacher. I really am sorry for your loss."

"You're the one who called her each year on Christmas eve. I'm Laurie her daughter."

"Laurie, it is nice to meet you and once again I'm sorry to hear of your mom's passing. I hope it is okay I called. To be honest I don't even know why I did. I just figured if anyone picked up it was someone close to her and I wanted to say how much I appreciated her back then and now."

"I know who you are," she said. "You are the one on TV and you were her favorite student."

I laughed out loud and said, "Laurie, trust me I don't think that is the case. I think I pretty much tormented her throughout that entire year."

"You don't remember me do you," she asked?

"I'm sorry? ...Excuse me?"

"We were in the same grade."

Back then in Indiana if a school was big enough to have multiple classes of the same age a teacher's child was always taught by another teacher. Call it fear of nepotism if you will, but it was the rule. Oh, I remembered a Laurie Wilson but never made the correlation between her last name and that of my teacher. Was she the same Laurie Wilson I could never forget? Brown hair and the greenest eyes I had ever seen. She was my first crush. I had even mustered up the courage to give her a Valentine's Day card that year in the sixth grade. It was the only one I ever gave out during all my years in elementary school and remember I had more years in primary school than most kids. It was the only one I wished to give out and it took me two days to be willing to take the risk.

"If you are the Laurie Wilson, I remember I think, … I might have given you a Valentine's Day card," I said, fully knowing I had.

"I remember."

I laughed. "How would you remember that?"

"Because you gave it to me the day after Valentine's Day."

"Well, I was the slow kid back then, remember?" I chuckled hoping to break the tension. "I had no idea she was your mother?"

"I remember you were sweet and always so polite," she said, and we talked for another hour catching up on almost three decades. Connecting the dots on an unexpected circle. She was married with two children and had become a teacher like her mom. We traded a few more stories and common memories of way back then but the one story I did not repeat was that she was my first kiss. Doing so would have been inappropriate plus she had probably forgotten the memory a long time ago. It happened on the playground. I had told my best friend Robert Riedel I was going to give her the card, but he told me she was out of my league and would probably tear it up. But she didn't. Instead, she read it and gave me a little peck right on the lips. Right there in front of everyone. My parents had worked very hard to impress upon me the idea that I could accomplish anything I put my mind to, but it was little Laurie Wilson who made me feel like anything was now possible. It was innocent but powerful. She had turned and walked away to go play with friends, but I remember standing there transfixed feeling like a champion and more confident than ever before in life. Thank God for the girls in the Wilson family both old and young. Both taught me a lot. No offense to her mother but those math questions I had memorized at age thirteen have long been forgotten but that kiss will always remain with me.

We hung up with her thanking me for the call saying it cheered her up after a tough week and me for saying thank you for the impact teachers make. Before hanging up, she called me Danny out of memory and reiterated how nice it was to have spoken after all these years. I did not feel the need to correct her, and it turns out there are many things in my past I would simply never wish to change.

That phone call came at Thanksgiving, and it started my own tradition of making phone calls during the December holiday. All of which came from a Christmas card sent to my long-gone mother by the toughest teacher I ever knew. Calls of thank you and appreciation unabashed and without regret to work associates, friends, and family to simply remind them of their value in my life. I think of them as a requirement of kindness in return for all I have been given.

It is what Christmas is all about though. Isn't it?

Chapter 6

Christmas Begins Long Before Christmas

The true spirit of the holiday doesn't always start in December. Sometimes it starts a few months earlier in the fall; when the air starts to grow crisp, and a young boy can see his breath in the air before dawn while folding newspapers on a familiar and cold garage floor. Christmas spirit is a commitment not a date on a calendar. I learned that lesson while tucking one end of newspapers into the other so a rubber band is not needed to keep the morning news intact while tossing them on the front porch of a hundred and fifty houses before six AM. I was thirteen and it was October. A few weeks before my fourteenth birthday. In 1974 in the state of Indiana one had to be fourteen in which to get a work permit and a paper route, and it took the signature of a guardian or parent to get one. A boy growing up in those days in the Midwest learned the lessons of responsibility early on. The northern suburbs of Indianapolis back then were a mix of farmland and new construction as urban sprawl got its first legs. I approached my mother, who for some reason I always seem to remember her at the kitchen sink with an apron on and doing dishes. "Mom, I want to get a paper route."

Before she asked why she said, "People count on getting their papers each day, Danny and not just on the days when it is not raining or snowing outside. It takes a serious commitment and one you can't put off just because you don't want to get up one morning. When you take on a responsibility, you're making a promise to others and choosing to disappoint others after giving someone your word is considered one of God's greatest sins."

I had not considered sin. I was thirteen and still yet to consider much more than what I had thought was a logical answer to my current dilemma and what I thought was a brilliant solution. A lot of things in my life are like that while looking back. All children tend to think in terms of small circles influenced only by what they know at their age. Now that my hair or what is left of it is gray, I can look back at how much larger those circles were and the impact of my parents' kindness and faith. After a solemn promise of dependability, she wiped her hands on her apron and then and only then, she asked me why I wanted a paper route?

"For Christmas," I told her. "I want to buy my own presents." She knew what I meant without asking and understood I did not mean toys for myself but to be able to afford to purchase gifts for my family on my own. My three older sisters and my older brother. Her, and Dad. There was no continued lecture on responsibility and no premonitions of how hard the work might be for one so young. She took me at my word with the single promise I had made and two weeks later I had a paper route. That is called faith.

Allow me to back track. Again, in the state of Indiana back then one must be fourteen to get a work permit and I was three weeks shy of my needed birthday. I didn't understand paperwork and to be honest I would have struggled to read whatever forms were necessary. I had not considered districts and territories or had even thought of how or even when a route might become available, but I found myself with a paper route in my own neighborhood. The last paper I would deliver each morning was to my own house and I never once gave it a thought as to how or why, ...or who. Small circles of thinking while influenced by a larger circle of love.

Unbeknownst to me and undisclosed by my father until almost forty years later and only when asked did he confess that he had a hand in the matter. I did not grow up with money and I most remember my father working long days and long hours to feed five hungry mouths. He sold insurance and had worked his way up to middle management which meant training new agents during the day and sales calls during the evening. I've already mentioned missed little league games and there were more than a few elementary school recitals, but this is not an admonishment. When truly needed he never failed to support.

When my mother approached him with my brilliant plan of a paper route he had balked. "He's too young Irene. He is already struggling in school. He doesn't need another distraction in his life. Let's keep him focused on his future and working through his challenges so he can get a real job one day."

"This is a job Frank and I agree he needs to learn those lessons. I think the earlier he understands them the better off he will be. Frank, he gave me his word and I know it will be tough, but he deserves a chance to prove to himself he can do it." With those words my father waited up the next morning in boxer shorts and a t-shirt to greet our current paper boy when he placed the morning paper inside our screen door. He made him an offer. A sixteen-year-old boy who was long tired of getting up at four AM and lugging papers in the dark. "How would you like to take the next three months off and still get paid? My son wants a paper route, and I don't want him delivering papers outside the neighborhood. If it doesn't work out, you get the route back. What do you say?"

The paper route was never mine. My father had signed his name as the one who had made the commitment to The Indianapolis Star to deliver 152 newspapers 7 days a week. It included weekends and especially Sundays which were the toughest days to any paper boy with all the circulars and ads which had to be placed in the middle. Sunday papers were always twice as thick and twice as heavy. Dad already had a litany of responsibilities and commitments to others and adding a paper route to the list must not have been something he enjoyed but he never grouched or complained. Nor did he allow me to do so either. A promise is a promise in the Midwest. He did sit me down at the kitchen table the evening I asked my mother for a route which is where all serious and adult matters were discussed between family. His tone was firm as he explained the full scope of the undertaking. No days off. No sleeping in late and no whining. He painted a picture of pure drudgery with descriptions of dark scary mornings with howling winds and driving rain as a small child trudged through the blackness, (we had streetlights,) alone to survive in the wilderness. He only left out the part about werewolves and possible bear attacks; those I conjured up in my own head. (By the way, I don't think there has been a bear sighting in Indianapolis since the days of Daniel Boone, but it did not matter.) My mind was made up. I needed money for Christmas, and this was the only way I could think of to get it. He then did something he had never done before. He stood from the table and extended his hand, and we shook on it because that is what real men do. As an adult I can't tell you how many contracts written on paper I have signed over the years because there have been too many to count. I also try not to focus on how many times in business ventures the ones who drew up the document failed to hold up to their end of the agreement. Sadly, it is why I now have a small team of lawyers on retainer. I still believe a handshake is a sacred bond and, in that moment, he treated me as an adult. He took me at my word. I don't know what level of faith he had in me in the moment, but he was willing to give it a try.

Those first few weeks while sitting on the garage floor folding papers in the cold were a test. I was still underage without knowing anything behind the scenes and my father would wake me up to walk to the end of the driveway when the box truck emblazoned with the local papers name would pull up and drop off several stacks of newspapers bound in twine or wire. He never once offered to assist in carrying them to the garage and only once he had to mention, "This was your idea Danny, remember that."

He did teach me though how to fold them and then how to load fifty papers in the front end of the canvas pouch and then another fifty in the back. It was slung over your shoulders with your head sticking out of a hole in the middle and when the front ran out you swung it around to the back to get more. Even at that age I wondered why the carry bag the Indianapolis Star had provided even bothered to print their name in orange glitter on it when no one was awake to see the advertising. "Carry your heaviest load early on when fresh and you have the strength, Danny. Then when you come back for the rest of the load it is all downhill and easier and faster." On Sundays they were loaded into a metal cart and either pulled by hand or on my bicycle. My father in his meticulous handwriting and engineering prowess had drawn out a map of our subdivision along with houses marked with X's for those who had subscribed to the morning paper and empty for those who had not. If you knew my father you would not be surprised, he had it laminated. Those of you much younger than myself may not know the term lamination. Seems like there are a lot of terms from those days people no longer use like cassette tape and station wagon. No one referred to it as a land line back then it was simply called the telephone and we only had one and it was bolted to the kitchen wall. I remember when it was a big deal when we upgraded from rotary to the new push button, "princess," phone.

Lamination is the process of taking any piece of paper and pressing it between two sheets of thin clear plastic and heating it until said piece of paper was enshrouded in a protective barrier even ancient Egyptian embalmers and mummy makers would have envied. There is something to be said about permanence. I still have my original laminated Social Security card in my wallet which was issued in 1973 and it is no worse for wear.

Sadly, it seems today everything is designed with planned obsolescence in mind but when you are a child you believe things will always be the same. Like paper routes. How many kids do you know today who have one? I wonder how many lessons are lost simply because people now choose the internet for information instead of tactile pages of cheap tissue paper thin pages with the smell of black ink I will never forget.

Luckily in those days people read the morning paper and reading my father's map required math and memorization. Seven houses in a row with an X and then one without. Another three in a row to be delivered before skipping one and then continuing on. I carried his map for months and continued to check it often while many times counting on my fingers between houses and rechecking it to make sure I had been correct. I had not forgotten my mother's words about commitment and just wanted to do it without disappointment. Looking back the mental process was more taxing than the physical but my legs and back grew stronger and so did my confidence.

For three weeks he walked every step of the route with me. Supervised my work. Gave me advice on just how to throw them from a distance to an exact spot on a front porch but he made me carry the load myself. On my fourteenth birthday and the day my work permit was valid I did the entire job by myself but thinking back he was sitting at the kitchen table at 5:30 AM in his boxer shorts waiting for me to return safely. I was frightened out there alone. The first morning on my own terrified me without him walking by my side but fear is a relative thing, and the fear of failure was greater than shadows and stray noises. I think it is an important lesson and one many in younger generations have yet to learn. There were no participation trophies in my youth. I have never had an employer who handed out accolades without performance as a measuring stick of success or failure. I never had a relationship which offered credit just for being present either. The numerical list of failures in my life more than outnumber the successes but those failures taught me perhaps even more then the wins. It also made the wins that much sweeter.

I never had an alarm clock when I was younger. I look back now almost ashamed that my wishes impacted my mother and father in so many ways, but I never missed a route in two and a half years. Like most children I went to bed each night forgetting what others do for you each day. My mother set her alarm for 4:00 AM and it was my father who woke me up and got me started.

Did you know Walt Disney's first job was that of being a paper boy? Or Bob Hope, John Wayne, Martin Luther King, and super model Kathy Ireland? It's true. I mentioned Kathy Ireland because these messages are not just for young boys who grew up in my home state. I admit my affinity for Indiana, but I hope the message is clear. Hard work is a virtue and when taught early on it spills over into every aspect of later years. As a child she saw an ad in her local Santa Barbara newspaper looking to hire couriers with the words, "Are you the right boy?" She wrote the editor of the paper stating that, "No, I am not the right boy, but I am the right girl, and I can do anything boys can do." She got the job and did it for longer than I did.

The Christmas of '74 was very special to me. I had only delivered papers for about eight weeks before holiday shopping began, (there was no such thing as Christmas in July in those days, and much like the concept of bottled water, it would have been scoffed at by most rational adults,) and for the first time I had money in my pocket I had earned all by myself. Or at least I had thought so at the time. I do not remember any gifts I might have received that year because it was the giving which made me the happiest. The excitement and anticipation of watching my family reaching for a gift I had paid for and wrapped myself.

When I was younger it was the anticipation of the holiday which created the most excitement. For me it still does. On that year it was not the arrival of Santa Claus which created the excitement for I had come to understand certain truths. It was the hope of making my family happy with something my efforts and hard work had brought to fruition. A lot of things started to make sense. Those long, lonely walks early in the morning with a heavy newspaper bag over my shoulders had all been worth it. I had been faced with a dilemma, came up with a solution, and worked hard to achieve a resolution to the problem. Which is pretty much the basic definition of becoming an adult. Is it not? Thinking I had done it all on my own was revised in my memory after a few more years but it did feel good. I learned more about self-confidence and tenacity while walking through the rain or snow in an Indiana winter than I ever did in most classrooms. There are a few exceptions, and I will tell them to you if you're willing to continue reading on.

The classic cliché of giving being better than receiving is not far from the truth. When you are a child, one tends to think of the holiday as being only about themselves. I am not saying young children are self-centered. Well, maybe I am just a little, but it takes a while to fully understand what Christmas really means and all it encompasses. It's quite an eye opener when you discover the gift itself is only part of the giving process when attempting to show how much you care. The back story of all it took to make it happen is as much a part of the equation as the gift itself. I'm glad I learned that part of the lesson when I was young but like many things in my life it took a bit longer to understand the complete picture. A child feels the need to brag about early successes and I wish I hadn't felt that need back then but I did. My family allowed me to be the hero that year and with admittance it felt wonderful.

Each opened their presents and gushed and yet none of the gifts were exceptional. Any gifts I received that year have long been lost to memory and I'm okay with that. It wasn't about the get; it was about the give. I was smiling as each of my siblings opened their gifts. So were my parents. Taking credit for the generosity came without thought and the hugs indeed felt like success. Factoring in a dependable wakeup call each morning never came to mind. Or the advice, or the faith in a fourteen-year-old boy whose track record had a larger list of disappointments than accomplishments. I learned dependability and the value of hard work. I found giving to be every bit as satisfying as receiving and like most lessons taught at Christmas time it would still take me some time to realize most important epiphanies don't really come from within ourselves. They come from the examples taught from those around us. Some gifts in life you simply cannot put a price tag on.

Chapter 7

The Night I Became Santa Claus

There were a lot of changes in the Hughes house the next year. My sister Nancy went off to Purdue University to study micro-biology in the fall of '75. My older brother moved out to be on his own. It left my sister Diane who was a year older than me and Mom and Dad. Diane was excited to have a room to herself. But I had not been looking forward to sleeping in a room by myself for the first time in my life. Back in those days there were small plug-in nightlights with 2-watt bulbs, and I bet they still make them, but I haven't seen one in years. We had one in the upstairs hallway and another in the bathroom I shared with my sister. After the first night I took the one in the bathroom and put it in my bedroom. I had not asked for permission, nor did I wish to admit I was afraid. My father who never missed anything in our house never said a word, but I know he noticed.

Three nights later or mornings depending on how you see it; at 4:00 AM it is difficult to differentiate between the two, my mother woke me up for the usual paper route. I found it unusual it was her and not him as was the norm. "How did you sleep," she asked. "I slept fine, why do you ask?" "I have been coming in here each night to turn off that night light Dan. You didn't need it, you just thought you did. Sometimes those things we think are our greatest weaknesses actually turn out to be our greatest strengths, Dan. Don't try so hard, just be yourself. Put the nightlight back in the bathroom before your dad notices it is missing. Okay. It's time to get up."

I hadn't even noticed. I had woken up in the same darkness I delivered papers in each morning and had even come to enjoy the quietness and stillness of early mornings when the rest of the world was asleep. In some ways it had become my own personal time. As I walked my brain was allowed to think of anything which might have popped into my head without a teacher scolding me for daydreaming instead of studying. Dyslexics tend to let their minds wander when the task at hand seems daunting. I only hope I can explain this in a way which makes sense. I had always felt different than most others and never had it been a good feeling. I was hoping only to fit in to other's expectations and not to be unlike everyone else. Yet on those early morning walks with fifty pounds of papers on my back I *was* different than everyone else. I couldn't compete on the same level in the daylight rat race but at 4:00 AM and while everyone else slept I was accomplishing something when they were doing nothing. I talked to squirrels with a certain type of kinship knowing they too were up early. I spoke with words such as, "How yah doing little buddy. I hope you have a good day."

Studying had never been my strong suit, but my curiosity and memory have always been keen. If something popped into my head during my route or I thought of a question I did not know the answer for I would remember it for later. My parents had a partial set of encyclopedias on a bookshelf in our family room and I would take a few minutes to look up things before grabbing a few more minutes of sleep before school. On one morning I surprised myself by recognizing the fact that squirrels don't all look alike and I wanted to know why?

In those days the grocery store offered individual volumes of The Encyclopedia Britannica to those who spent enough money there each month. With five kids to feed my parents always made the cut. My mother was always strong in mind and will but, often frail in body and I remember several times when she was confined to bed for weeks at a time. On those occasions my father took over the role of grocery shopping and he never asked for the latest volumes, so I missed out on volumes L.M.N.O. and P. but did you know there are ten different types of Squirrels in the United States? It's true. Most of the little fellas I saw were Eastern Gray Squirrels. Every once in a while, I would come across a Fox Squirrel which is the largest tree squirrels in the United States. I had tried to look it up but again sounding out words never made much sense to me. I looked under S, but the second letter Q threw me off. I tried S, K, without any luck. Remembering that sometimes the letter C makes the same sound as a K, I turned the pages back hoping to find a photo but again to no avail. Never thought to look for a stupid Q.

For the record I never saw much sense in the letter Q to begin with. I think it was added to the English language by some pompous and arrogant know-it-all for the sole purpose of showing off. We already have the K and the C, which pretty much sound the same, so do we really need a third? Why make Wheel of Fortune more difficult than it already is? Grammar was always more about the rules than common sense and those who tend to set the guidelines love nothing more than to point out when someone else is wrong. Even words which start with the actual sound of the letter Q like the word *cute* are not even spelled with a Q? How is that possible? Make it simple. Why make life difficult? No wonder immigrants to our country find our language so hard to understand and learn? I was born here and still sometimes struggle. I'm telling you I could eliminate several letters from your keyboard if you listened to reason. The word *cutie* should simply be spelled QT. Sound it out. I just saved you three letters and some printer ink, but no one is listening to reason.

There are only about a hundred and twenty words in the entire English language which start with the letter X, so I say get rid of that one too. We don't need the redundancy. EKS does the job nicely sound wise and we can get rid of another letter on the payroll which spends most of its time sitting around doing nothing waiting to be called into the game. In a day of corporate downsizing why should unnecessary letters like X get a reprieve? Oh, I know, pharmaceutical companies would not be happy for it is their favorite letter by far when making up fancy names for new products. I don't know why? Doesn't X or EX mean formerly? As in no longer current or viable in the context. Like ex-husband or excommunicated. Yet, pharmaceutical companies love the letter X. ExLax is a trusted medicine for constipation and has been sold for over a hundred years in America. Wow, they used two X's in that one, it must be good. Still, they could have called it Colon Blow and forgone the use of two X's and provided the consumer with an even better idea of what the product actually does.

It bothers me the way we are forced to spell and pronounce words. And it has nothing to do with my dyslexia. Those who originally wrote the rules expect everyone else in the world to have an exasperated knowledge of etymology or the history of words and where they come from in order to attempt to spell them today. Most of use just want to finish a sentence without the help of spell check. For crying out loud! Some of us have lives. The word xylophone starts with the letter X! And everyone knows xylophone starts with a Z sound with no X sound in it anywhere!

If I were a showoff know-it-all, which I am not, I would point out to you the word xylophone which was coined in 1886 comes from the Greek "xylon" which means wood, plus "phone" which means sound, but who cares! (And according to the rules you are not supposed to start a sentence with the word *and,* but I just did it twice in the last paragraph and once in this sentence and you probably didn't even notice. I did it just to piss off English teachers.) Don't let the rules get in the way of a good story.

Sorry. I might have gotten on a rant there and I apologize for the ADHD. Anyway, back to the story. At breakfast I asked my mom how you spelled the word squirrel, and she told me, and I wrote it down letter for letter to read up on them later after school. I still laugh out loud when I see a Disney cartoon with a dog in it who cannot pay attention and it is usually a squirrel which precipitated such. I am that dog. I am pretty sure my former employer would not be so happy if they knew my disdain for the Q after all these years, but I am who I am.

I remember my father once telling me around that time, "There were two types of people who did well financially in life, those who were willing to do what others were not, and those who were capable of doing what others cannot do."

I told you my mother was the smartest person I knew but my father might have been the wisest. I thought of his words one morning when still less than halfway through my route on a morning when it started to rain unexpectedly. I hadn't worn a raincoat and it did not take long to become soaked, but I continued on. I finished the first and longest loop and when I got home to refill my bag with the last one third of the route it didn't make much sense to put on rain gear when I was already wet, so I loaded my sack and stepped back into the rain smiling. Everyone else in the neighborhood was asleep. I had two doctors on my route and even one of the teachers who taught at the middle school I attended but they were not up and working at that hour. Like my father had said I was doing what they were not willing to do. The usual pressures of schoolwork were absent, and I enjoyed the repetition. There was a peace in being alone and walking through the darkness I hadn't recognized before. I was in my own element and one I was comfortable in for the first time. Almost anyone could have walked that route, but I was the one who chose to do it.

I also liked to think that perhaps while others slept and I walked in the darkness, I was closer to God with less competition. I had several conversations with him on early mornings. I said conversations not prayers because prayers tend to be requests asked for when wishing for something or in times of great need and often tend to become pleads for mercy, but these were neither. We just talked. Well, I talked but I always thought he was listening. I was happy and had been taught even though there were struggles or challenges or work to be done faith would see you through. I will never be an early morning person and would prefer to stay up late at night to write instead of rising before the sun, but early mornings have paid the bills now for many years. For over seventeen years I co-hosted a morning show on TV which required a three AM wakeup call Monday through Friday. It was not a wakeup call I looked forward to, but the paycheck often dictates the rules.

Overcoming one's fears or obstacles is not a matter of ignoring them. It is a simple mathematical equation of plus or minus and greater or lesser than. Or as I referred to them back then as your goes intos and your take aways. You count your strengths and decide if they are greater than your weaknesses.

It is amazing what one can overcome. Fears change from generation to generation but back in the mid 1970's if you asked most anyone, they would have listed their first as public speaking. It was long before the days of social media and YouTube sensations or TikTok influencers where just about everyone has had at least their own fifteen minutes of attention or their own podcast. When my own biggest fears at the time involved walking to a chalk board in front of a small classroom the thought of one day being on national television for over thirty years in front of millions of people each day was never an expectation or even a thought process. Yet it has been my reality all these years. Funny how sometimes pathways lead us to destinations we never thought as possible.

Those first few weeks delivering papers before Christmas the year before were in many ways my first steps into adulthood. I didn't make enough money in '74 to be required by tax laws to file a return but in 1975 I had worked all year and my father sat me down in December before the tax man could come calling. Again, at the kitchen table. "Danny part of any job is making sure you put aside some of what you earned for the government." My father being my father thought it pertinent to do my taxes before the year end instead of waiting until April like everyone else. He liked to wrap things up at year's end in a neat little package and was not one to procrastinate on anything.

"Wait, what?"

"It's called taxes Dan, and everyone needs to pay them son."

I was not happy when my father sat me down to do the paperwork. "Why do they get part of my money? They didn't get up at four in the morning and in the dark to deliver papers! That's not fair I told him."

"Dan you will find there are a lot of things in adult life which don't seem fair, but it is why I told you not to spend all your money."

In my first full year of delivering papers, I had earned $1264 dollars and 64 cents or roughly 23 dollars a week. The first check I ever wrote was with a bank account set up by my parents and it was to the I.R.S. After a lengthy explanation of taxes,

I asked my father why he wanted to pay it now instead of waiting until April and his answer has always stuck with me.

"A man doesn't wait to pay his financial obligations until it is convenient, Danny or wait until the last minute. If you have the money, you pay it. Otherwise, your bills will always control you instead of you controlling them. Never let your debts own you."

"So, it always rains on April fifteenth then?" He looked a bit perplexed by my question. "You told me to save my money for a rainy day?" My father laughed.

That year at Christmas our family traditions changed a bit. Nancy was home from college and Don was there for Christmas Eve but stayed at his new place before returning in the morning for Christmas day. My oldest sister Janet had not returned home for Christmas since the story I told you before but, in her defense, she had since married and started a family of her own. My sister Diane who is a year older than me was excited to share a bedroom with Nancy for the night since I was the only other sibling at home, and I usually just irritated the heck out of her.

It was the first year we decorated the tree as a family. It has always been Santa's responsibility to do so when us children were asleep awaiting his arrival. My father had retrieved the ornaments from the attic and placed the boxes in designated stacks on our fireplace hearth. They were separated by age and importance, and it was my mother who determined their placement in those piles. I was always amazed at how my mother's favorites seemed eggshell fragile yet had been in our family for so long. A child's understanding of longevity is measured only in terms of a few years but many of those ornaments had been in her family for generations. She would handle them with a reverence usually associated with religious artifacts or museum pieces and I guess to her they were both. I look back in retrospect on how our Christmas tree and everyone else's is a personal history lesson of those who lived within their own walls. Each ornament conjures up remembrances. At Christmas time we all think of memories. We reminisce about the good times and even when touched by thoughts of sadness for those who are no longer with us during the holiday we tend to concentrate on warm thoughts.

I didn't understand it at the time, but I do now. She would gently pull a mouth blown glass ornament from before her childhood from the box and hold it up deep in thought before handing it to my father to place it at the top of the tree. He did not need to ask. She need not tell him where it should go. He knew not to place it low enough on the tree for prying and curious hands. Usually, mine. Most of those ornaments are still in our family which in and of itself is a miracle with five children in the family. The benefit of having only one child is parents always know who broke something. Those of you with children understand what I mean.

My mother played Christmas carols on the organ and the rest of us decorated the tree as Dad handed out ornaments to each one of us in a systematic and well thought out process of where each should go. It felt good to be surrounded by family and trimming the tree became a new yet time honored joy. We strung popcorn and cranberries into lengths of garland. I drank cocoa until I had a chocolate hang over and by 10:00 PM I was spent and fell asleep on the coach. Newspapers still needed to be delivered on Christmas morning back then, and it was my father who awoke me at midnight, still on the sofa and covered by a blanket.

"Is it time?"

"No, not yet. I could use your help though he said. I will make you a deal. You help me and I will help you with your route and we can get it done in half the time. Sound good?"

"What do you need?"

"I need you to be Santa Claus," he told me.

"What?"

"The family is together so let's make this year special, what do you say?"

I did not understand. I had come to understand the difference between childhood visions and reality and as much as I adored Christmas and always will his comment had made little sense to me. "Who do you really think Santa Claus is," he asked me?

"Dad, I'm not a kid anymore I know it's you and Mom."

"You're partially right Danny but there is a lot more to it than just that. Do you remember how when you were little and on Christmas morning you would find boot marks from the fireplace hearth and all over the living room around the tree?"

I laughed. I had already figured out perhaps a few years before they had been his. Boot marks. He had stepped into a baking pan of flour and left them there for me to see. Those footprints had been noticeably absent for a while now with both Mom and Dad thinking they were no longer as enchanting or necessary. "I know you're smart enough to know who left them there, but you have never called me out for it. Why is that? You know our policy in this house about honesty, yet you never once pointed them out even when you knew the truth?"

"You did it to make me excited, I told him. You did it to make me happy and I understand."

"Yes, I did, and I wish you could have seen your eyes through mine when you would come downstairs and see those snowy footprints on the carpet. Your eyes always got so big! Seeing you so excited always made your mother smile. Even in years when it hadn't snowed it fooled you every time," and he laughed.

I laughed out loud myself realizing he was correct. I had wanted to believe. It was part of the magic and he had always provided just enough for a young one to do so willingly. "Everyone has to grow up some time, but it doesn't have to mean the magic is no longer real or important," he went on to say. "We are all Santa," my father told me. He is inside all of us. Doing things to make others smile and happy is what the holiday is all about. You kids are all grown now but let's make your mom smile once again. She has had a rough year. What do you say?" It was the Christmas of my 7th grade year and shortly after, she had been diagnosed with lung cancer.

He took me down to the basement and I helped him carry what packages there were back up into the living room. He shared his wisdom by telling me to remember to wrap those presents marked from Santa in all the same wrapping paper but different from any of the gifts from family. "You were always observant Danny, and it might have given it away." He showed me how to stack presents along the fireplace hearth starting with the largest and then stacks of medium sized and then the smallest off to the side. I told you there were never large sums of gifts, but I will always remember the family room seemed absolutely filled with giftwrapped surprises of every shape and size spilling out into the room from under the tree. My father was meticulous and with his engineering mind he shared his secret with me early on Christmas morning. "You take the largest ones first; he said and fill the voids in front of the tree. Use up as much floor space as possible." He would point to one on the stack and I would retrieve it and hand it to him as he placed it and stood back to check his work. "Then take the medium sized ones and always lean them against the bigger ones so it takes up even more space and volume. If you pack them too tightly it doesn't look like as many packages." He then took the smallest ones and tucked them into any gaps and the room absolutely filled up. He stood back and moved a few from one place to another so no two had matching gift wrap side by side. When he was finished, he stood back and folded his arms with a look of satisfaction and a smile on his lips which I can never forget. In that moment he was every bit as much Santa Clause as anyone dressed in red.

He put his arm around my shoulder like so many other times and stood for a moment and then said, "What about your gifts, he asked? They're wrapped right?"

"Yes, they're upstairs!"

"Well, go get 'em."

I came back down with two gifts for each family member, and he told me to place them where I best thought they should go. I saved the smallest for last and told Dad, "This one is special! I picked it out for Mom myself. I hope she likes it."

"I'm sure she will. What is it?"

"I can't tell you. You will have to wait 'till morning to find out."

"It sounds very special indeed then," he said.

"It is Dad, it's the most important gift I have ever gotten anyone."

"Well then let's make it even more special. Wait here." He walked into the kitchen and came back with a pen and one of those gift cards which reads to and from. He also had a roll of Scotch tape. He instructed me to carefully remove the tag already on the gift so as not to tear the paper. I did so but didn't understand why. I had signed the original to Mom from Dan. "Here he said as he handed me the blank tag. Now, why don't you sign it with your new title. I think she would like that."

As I started to write he stopped me. I had almost printed the word Mom when he touched my shoulder and said, "I know it is difficult to think of your mother as anything other than mom, but she has been Irene since she was just a little girl, and every little girl likes to get a gift from Santa. Just trust me on this."

So, I did. It felt weird referring to her by her true name and I had never done it before in speech or especially in writing. To be honest I don't know how much time I had ever spent even thinking of her as a little girl before that moment. My father went on to say, "She wasn't Mom until you kids were born. You think she is a pretty good Mom?"

"Yeah, the best," I told him. "I agree, she is. She has earned the title just like you have earned the title of new Santa so don't screw it up. Okay?"

The card read to: Irene, from: Santa. I told dad I was a bit worried she might think the gift was from him, and he smiled. "She is pretty smart; I think she will figure it out." For the record that gift tag was also in the memory box of things my mother kept from all those years ago.

I still put packages around the tree in the very same manner as he taught me to do that night. Christmas is always what you chose to make of it, and I felt blessed then as I do now, he taught me how to do it. I have witnessed the same look of wonderment on my own daughter's face many times when she was little, and the room looked filled with gifts even though it was not the case.

The flour footprints leading from the fireplace to the tree were a bit smaller that year and I was honored to have put them there. Often times in my youth being chastised for not seeing the obvious was cause for me to sink into my shell but after dad and I had poured baking flour onto a cookie sheet dad had said, "No dummy. Santa doesn't wear tennis shoes. Go get your snow boots out of the hall closet!" I wasn't offended or even felt scolded for we were both a part of the same mission and getting it right was the only end goal. Life is all about the little details it turns out.

We walked the paper route that Christmas morning together. He had said it would only take half the time, but he had been wrong. We talked the whole way about past Christmases and when questioned he shared stories about his own holiday memories. He told me about one year during the great depression when his only gift was an apple. Yet he told the story with a smile. His father had handed him the apple while telling him it was the King's apple, and he would be king for the day. He could ask his father to do any one of his own chores, but he must take a big bite out of the apple before commanding such. Each chore requested by the newly appointed king required such a bite and once the apple was gone his reign as monarch was over. My father's father shoveled coal that Christmas from the coal chute into a bucket and fired up the furnace which had been my dad's first daily chore since the age of six. Granddad then dried dishes at breakfast and again at lunch time. He also set the table for Christmas dinner as well. After dinner and with only one bite left my father had run out of things to act upon as king but with a whisper in his ear from my grandmother my grandfather was requested by the king to dance a little jig in the kitchen much to my grandmother's delight. As my father told me the story, I could picture my grandfather who I only knew from sepia tone photographs because he had passed before my birth, kicking his heels up in what my mind conjured as depression age coveralls and worn work boots in a kitchen lit with kerosene lanterns instead of electricity. I am sure I got most of the details wrong in my head, but he told the story with such passion I could envision the faded wallpaper darkened by the soot of a wood fired stove and felt the laughter shared by my grandmother and my father as both laughed until they were forced to wipe tears from their eyes. The apple was not my father's gift at all. It was the moment. It is never just about the gifts alone.

That year was the first in memory where someone had to wake me to start the festivities. When my mother saw the snowy footprints, she smiled. "It looks like Santa had a party down here!" I had requested to Dad that Mom open her special gift last. He had told me to hide it in the tree. It was small. My mom always loved roses. They were her absolute favorite. Dad had even planted her a rose garden many years earlier in a raised bed along the side of the house and lining our driveway so she would see them every day when pulling in or going out. She spent hours out there tending to her flowers. My father was never much for gardening because he was so busy with work but when she fell ill, he took it upon himself to make sure they were well cared for.

I had walked our local mall from one end to the other looking for something perfect. I did not have anything in particular in mind I just knew I would know it when I saw it, and I did. At Zales Jewelers I saw it in the glass case and knew it was absolutely perfect. A small carved pink rose shaped pendant hanging from a delicate gold chain. When the salesclerk told me it was called rose quartz, I had to have it. When I asked her to see it closer, she said to me, "You might want to look at something less expensive kid." I didn't know back then why her comment bothered me so much, but it did. I had always been taught my manners especially when dealing with adults, but it was my first run in with arrogance and I told you before I don't like rudeness.

"No ma'am I am pretty sure that is what I want but I would just like to see it up close first."

"Kid I work on commission I don't have time for window shoppers." I knew what commission was. It was how my father made his living selling insurance. It's how I made money selling papers. "I know what commission is, I told her. How much is it?" The price tag was right next to it but $89.98 is a lot of nines and a lot of eights and both were tough back then. She didn't say what she was thinking but I had seen the same face on some teachers faces before and so I simply walked away. I am not good with confrontation. I wasn't comfortable with it then and perhaps even less so today but instead of walking out I walked to another counter where a man in a fancy suit and tie was standing. "Sir, do you work on commission?"

"Excuse me?"

"Sir, I asked if you work on commission?"

"Why, yes, but."

"Would you like to sell a necklace today?" he walked with me back to the counter and I pointed saying it was the one I wanted. "How much is it sir?"

"It's about ninety-three dollars with tax, give or take a few cents."

"Thank you it is perfect, and I thank you for your time. I will take it." I pulled a hundred-dollar bill from out of my blue jeans pocket and laid it on the counter while looking the sales lady straight in the eye. "Would you like us to gift wrap it for you sir the man said, it doesn't cost any extra?"

"I would appreciate that very much, thank you again."

I walked out of the jewelry store with my perfect gift and waved to the sales lady with the scowl on her face on the way out. I don't think she was happy the nice man in the suit had asked her to wrap it.

When mom opened it, she put her hand over her mouth, but her eyes were smiling. Then teared up. From that day forward she never took it off. It never left her neck and although she is no longer with us, I like to think the necklace is still with her. Mom was buried with only two pieces of jewelry. The wedding ring she wore for the thirty-seven years my parents were married and the necklace I gave her that year at Christmas. I said so with no sense of sadness for she has been gone now for forty years. Plus, I prefer to think of fond memories and her smile that Christmas morning instead. It was the year I became Santa Claus.

Chapter 8

Unexpected Christmas Opportunities

Throughout my life Christmas has either inspired me or dictated part of my future. It was never part of any master plan it just always seemed to work out that way. It was a time of year which always felt differently than any other. As a school child it meant a break from the classroom. As an adult it meant putting other things aside for a bit and concentrating purely on family and friends. Not that family is ignored throughout the rest of the year it's just sometimes the responsibilities of work and paychecks can often become first in our minds when trying to provide for those who we love. I think as a child I always felt somewhat disappointed when the holiday was over, and it meant stepping back into reality. Without knowing it a part of me was looking for a way to keep the spark alight throughout the year.

Growing up in a family where your mother was a musical prodigy meant music was always a part of my life. Musical ability though is closely assimilated with the math centers of the human brain so playing any type of instrument myself was never in the cards. Even with the best of intentions all attempts at learning the trumpet and then piano or organ never proved to be successful. Even with my limitations I still believe I was born with many blessings although a decent singing voice is not one of them. Nevertheless, on the wall of my office resides a gold record with my name on it. Don't be impressed. You haven't heard the story yet.

When I was younger, there was nothing I enjoyed more during the holiday than listening to Christmas music while I fell asleep. Those of you younger than myself may not remember a marvelous invention created by the Kenner Toy Company in the 1970's called the "Close and Play Phonograph." It was amazing. You could stack a half-dozen 45 RPM records on the spindle and when you closed the lid which housed the stylus it would play your records in succession and then turn itself off. I loved that record player.

My favorite Christmas tune was recorded back in the 1950's by a man much like myself. He was not a musician or a singer and only recorded one record, but it too went gold and in fact his sold over a million copies. The fact a 1987 survey of the most hated Christmas tunes listed his release at the top of the list doesn't bother me because I loved the song. I wonder if it bothered him. Carl Weisman was a Danish recording engineer with a passion for ornithology. He recorded songbirds in the wild using captured Nazi Magnetic recording equipment after the war and in doing so many times his recordings would be interrupted by the sound of barking dogs. He spliced the barking sounds together and set them to music and in 1955 he released the 45 RPM single, "Jingle Bells by The Singing Dogs." I bet you have heard it more than once at Christmas time. Call me immature but the song still makes me laugh. Laughter is good. Right?

I have always surrounded myself with those who were smarter or even more talented than myself. It's not a bad lesson to learn and one I highly recommend. No one succeeds on their own. Those who think they are self-made individuals are yet to learn one of life's most important messages. In my young adult years and more by serendipity than anything else I found myself in a circle of local musicians and entertainers. I enjoyed their company, and they enjoyed my sense of humor. A lesson learned early on in life was making others laugh tended to lessen the severity of the harassment on the playground and even allowed me to bond with others. Being known as the funny kid felt much better than other adjectives I had been labeled with before.

In 1982 more as a joke than anything else I talked some friends of mine into recording a song to be entered into a contest held by local radio station Q-95 WFBQ. The classic rock station allowed listeners to submit what they called, "sub-basement," tapes which if funny enough would be played on the air. Those of us who grew up in Indianapolis are extremely proud of our hometown and we look for occasions to celebrate where we are from. The first contest was to submit a song surrounding the Indianapolis 500. So, we did. Looking back the song was immature and politically incorrect; wrought with double entendres and sexual inuendo toeing a line the FCC could not complain about but any human resources department today would most certainly take umbrage with it. Risking the current climate of cancel culture forty years later the premise was an ode to Indy driver superstar Mario Andretti written from the vantage point of a secret admirer. Mario hated that song, but the listeners and radio jocks Bob and Tom loved it, and we won the contest hands down. The song was played on the air that month of May over 100 times.

For one who never sought the limelight it was my first taste at any notoriety, and it felt good. Since I was the one who wrote the lyrics and fronted the band more by talking my way through songs than singing, I was the one Bob and Tom directed most of their questions towards when interviewed in the radio station after winning the competition. I use the term, "band," loosely simply because the three truly talented musicians talked into this adventure were indeed serious and talented artists. They worked either together or in other bands which were booked heavily in the Indianapolis night club scene. They weren't looking to be attached to musical parody, yet the production value of everything we recorded was top notch and it was a big part of what garnered the audience reaction. We recorded twelve more songs over the next three years for Q-95 for every sub-basement tape competition and even submitted tapes they had not even asked for. We created songs for everything from back to school to national doughnut day and every time they got air play. If we submitted a tape, it became an anticipated event. For two or three days before playing a new song Bob and Tom would tease the audience while telling them to tune in later that week for our latest release. We weren't a real band at all. I was simply a hanger-on who had convinced some friends we could have some fun.

Allow me a few sentences to pay some homage to a few guys who had the same spirit of youthful ridiculousness and the bond which can be formed simply through laughter and time spent together. Gary Osborn in his twenties was a genius level sound engineer working for the RCA corporation. Gary had bought an old dilapidated Victorian house in what is now recognized in Indianapolis as the art district. I can't remember exactly but, I think it had six or maybe eight bedrooms. He rented them out to other musicians with low rent in return for labor to renovate the place. I never lived there but spent many weekends sanding oak flooring and pounding nails. In the basement he built an 18-channel recording studio outfitted with the most up to date recording equipment available. It became a destination for artists from around the Midwest to come and record. He was also a musical prodigy playing several instruments. But his true gift from God was producing.

Greg McGuirk was and still is a keyboard and synthesizer player whose fingers and ears were attached as if the same. You could hum a tune and he could play it flawlessly without practice or doubt. Pat Byrket should be a name every music lover knows simply because he had a voice and a look which personified 1980's rock and roll. I often wonder why some people make it and others do not. He deserved stardom. As a quiet guy when talking to him most people were shocked at his command when standing behind a microphone. His power and perfect pitch along with the ability upon request to sing in different octaves gave a harmonization to each channel of recording. This gave a depth to his volunteered background vocals far exceeding my best attempts at talking my way through the primary lyrics. They were the ones who inspired me and pushed me to the front of the stage without any sense of resentment or ego on their part. It was just four idiots enjoying the moment with me knowing I was not their equal. With them pushing me to write another song with lyrics which might be funny.

We spent hundreds of hours in that basement studio. I mostly sat on a couch in the corner just soaking up the sounds of exceptional talent as they rehearsed or recorded their own projects and play lists. At the end of an evening either Gary or Greg would look over and ask if I had anything I had come up with and they would spend additional time putting music to my often sophomoric lyrics. Always with the same intensity and focus they put on their own creations. After winning the first competition the radio station told us we needed a name to attach to the song and since Gary owned the house and the recording studio, we all felt it only fitting he should get top billing. So, it was. Our non-band which had never performed on any stage became known in Indianapolis as: "Gary Microwave and the Leftovers." Come on. You tell me that is not funny. A group of guys recording music purely to make others laugh and doing so with no intent of taking themselves seriously in the venture at all. No one, especially me ever thought it would amount to anything. It was about the fun along the way.

One late night in the studio after our usual clowning around Gary asked me to get in front of the microphone to record whatever childish lyrics we were working on at the time. It was in November 1985. I don't remember what Christmas parody we were working on, and it will always be lost to memory but what I will always remember thinking was Gary had not yet rolled tape when the aftereffects of a lukewarm Budweiser hit the gut of someone who rarely drank. Continued seconds ticked off the clock as an epic foamy eructation escaped from my lips and lungs. Eructation is the technical medical term for a belch and even with trying to impress you with big words I will bet you were less impressed than my buddies who doubled over in laughter. I had been wrong. Gary had rolled tape and recorded an epic twenty-two second burp which among my friends will always be legendary. He played the tape back a dozen times and each time it got funnier.

It was Greg the keyboard player who said, "We need to make that part of a song," and inspiration was born. Thinking back to Carl Weisman and my favorite Christmas song from childhood I asked the guys if they had ever heard it. All agreed they had. If dogs barking Jingle Bells could be a hit, then why not this? Gary patched the tape through Greg's keyboard and each key came out as a note of belching and we recorded our Christmas sub-basement tape for Q-95 in less than fifteen minutes. "Jingle Belch," became the number one requested song that year at Christmas. Bob and Tom shared the song with fellow disc-jockeys around the country and we got additional air play in several states. The next spring the radio station contacted us and asked us to be a part of a live concert they had sponsored for a local charity event, and I balked. No, balked is not the right emotion; I panicked.

Being behind a microphone in a basement sound studio or working as a DJ in a local hotspot disco club which I had done for over two years had pushed my comfort zone far beyond earlier expectations. Fronting a band in front of a live audience with spotlights was more than my confidence would allow. It was my friends who gave me no choice in the matter. They did not allow me to decide. Instead, they assured me they had my back, and we could do this and to trust them. Gary Microwave and the Leftovers was the headlining act that night and touted as their first ever live performance, but I was the only one who qualified in such a description. I threw up twice backstage before going on. When the band was introduced along with excessive fanfare from Bob and Tom, we received a standing ovation before our six song set even began. Apparently, radio airplay had made us a thing. In every interview we had ever done Gary had asked we not mention out last names simply because they were serious musicians and did not wish to be either labeled or tarnished by being associated with such ridiculousness. Seeing people in the crowd pointing to Gary, Greg and Pat and recognizing them from previous musical ventures was interesting. I was the only unknown entity but simply by standing next to those three gave me a level of credibility I had never earned. Gary started our set by shouting into the mic, "Tonight we are here to have some fun! Are you ready!"

I wasn't but he struck the first cord on his guitar and our part of the show began. We sang songs about farting and doughnuts and how cute Mario Andretti was with three-part harmony. Notice I said only three-part harmony because I was the fourth guy in the band. My contribution was poetically talking through the main lyrics with a 1980's FM disc jockey voice, which was not even my own, but well-rehearsed to cover the fact I could not sing. And it worked. Every song ended with uproars of applause and even audience members shouting out requests of one of the songs we had submitted to the sub-basement tapes. We ended our set with, "Jingle Belch." Which by the way cannot be performed live without the possibility of blowing out a spleen by the one attempting to belch so many notes in a two-and-a-half-minute song. Greg had it sampled in his synthesizer, and I lip synced the whole song while Pat and Gary added everything from church bells to Gregorian chants in the background. Spontaneously at the end of the song I threw in a little bit of drama into it and fell flat on my back from a standing position onto the stage as if from exhaustion and possible death. It hurt. A lot. I had not really thought through what the effects of a pratfall would entail and had knocked the wind out of myself. Comedians take risks and this one was worth it. When the song was over there was dead silence for several seconds and then the crowd erupted in a standing ovation of ill gained respect and adulation few people ever get to receive.

It was the first and only live performance of a band called, "Gary Microwave and the Leftovers," but once again the support of friends had pushed me past my comfort zone into something wonderful and unexpected. Gary got married later that year. Greg went on to become a highly successful studio musician and Pat, being Pat, simply went his separate way. Me, I moved to San Francisco to pursue a career in stand-up comedy. Before moving out west I told the guys I thought we should press "Jingle Belch," as a single and try to sell it and they told me it would never work. They knew the record industry and I did not, but I had seen the reaction the song had created and thought it worthy of a try. All three signed over their rights to the song for a dollar a piece and wished me the best.

After being rejected by every single record label in America I made the decision to press the song myself and start my own label. Convincing the Indianapolis Philharmonic Orchestra to do the musical tracks for free was another lesson in salesmanship. We had originally recorded the song with Greg tuning his keyboard sounding like a child's toy piano but having full orchestration just added to the ridiculousness of the tune. A hundred classically trained professional musicians who I had thought were potentially highbrow gave their time and expertise for two days in a concert hall while we recorded and laughed our way through the process. I released "Jingle Belch," in early November of 1988. Sending free copies to top jocks at two hundred and fifty top radio stations across the country got me air play. Doing the research to find out who those top jocks were and personalizing the letters attached scored some points and even garnered some new friends along the way. Asking them to ask their listeners to call local record stores asking if they carried the song certainly helped as well. I had pressed ten thousand 45 RPM's and every single one of them was sitting in boxes in my apartment. I had no distribution and no shipping department. Four hours a day were spent on the phone calling record stores in those top markets asking if they had received any requests for the song and many said they had, indeed. I started shipping boxes of ten records or maybe twenty. The largest order I had that year was to Phoenix where a local disc jockey played the song a lot. It was a hundred records. Each box had an invoice sheet, my newly printed business cards, and a personal letter of thank you. By mid-December there were no more boxes in my apartment. My wholesale price to the record store was two bucks and they sold it for four. With my shipping costs and phone bills along with the initial pressing costs, labeling and free samples I made a whopping three thousand and fifteen dollars in profit that year. Maybe the guys in the band were right.

The next year I pressed twenty-five thousand and it cut my production and pressing cost in half. I sent out five hundred copies to radio stations and then requested record stores pay for the shipping and handling. The previous year almost ten percent of the stores who committed to selling my song never paid me. It was a lesson learned and even with dyslexia I have always kept meticulous records. I have made a lot of mistakes in my life, but I don't tend to make the same one twice. The second year I did not sell the entire twenty-five thousand, but I got close.

The third year I was contacted by a record distributor, and we brokered a deal which paid me less on the sale of each record but freed me up to focus on other career goals without having to micro-manage every aspect of the project. It took seven years to amass enough sales to earn gold record status and if you call me a one hit wonder it won't hurt my feelings because it is true. It still meant accomplishing something few people could have predicted. No one ever got rich from the sale of the record, but it was enough for me to make the down payment on my first house. I am proud of that. My father telling me he was proud of me for not giving up meant even more. My father who always preached I should work towards getting, "a real job," played a record I recorded. which was nothing more than belching out loud, for our neighbors on the console stereo in the living room of the house I grew up in, while proudly commenting, "My son did that!" Ain't life itself funny sometimes?

Chapter 9

Christmas Surprises

My passion for the holiday and an inquisitive nature has led me to an unexpected hobby. One which has also led me to several opportunities I would never have forecasted. QVC is not only a television network but also one of the largest retail giants of our day. Fourth quarter is always a retailer's busiest time of year. It was also mine. From Thanksgiving to Christmas, I took no days off. Not because my employer required such, for they have always been generous with time off. I fully understand the importance of a sense of work-life balance. Usually starting in July or August my schedule starts to fill up with guest appearances on pod casts, blog requests and interviews to be either recorded or broadcast live during the holiday season. Without attempting to do so I have become a recognized unofficial Christmas historian. For me there is joy in doing the research. My mind has always tended to wonder towards the why. Even when daydreaming. Math equations were tough, but history of any kind was simply memorization. History was always the one subject in school which never seemed too difficult. It wasn't enough though. Knowing what people have done over time wasn't the same as understanding why they did it. Christmas time has always made me feel different than any other time of year. I wanted to know why. Learning as much as I could about the why of our observances meant more to me than just following them. I have never asked for or been paid for those appearances. With the exception of the before mentioned novelty song and this book and a company I owned and operated back in the mid-90's called White Christmas, which offered high end custom Christmas lighting here in Philadelphia and surrounding areas. I never intended my passion to draw additional income.

No one likes a know-it-all but let's be honest, everyone enjoys being considered an expert on something. Especially when at a younger age no one thought I knew much of anything. Wanting to learn everything I could about the holiday both religious and secular became a pleasant obsession which I still indulge myself in today. Traveling to Jerusalem, Galilee and Bethlehem and walking on the same soil Jesus might have walked on two thousand years ago tends to take any book whether it be a history textbook or the bible itself and transforms words on a page to a personal and deeply emotional connection.

Author Malcom Gladwell once stated in his bestselling book Outliers: The Story of Success, "it takes ten thousand hours of practice to become a master or expert in any endeavor," but he was wrong. Sure, it is a catchy phrase and one which is easy to remember but dedicating countless hours to something you're not passionate about or simply not gifted in seems like a waste of valuable time. I could have studied algebra all this time and I am still not sure I could pass the math portion of the S.A.T.'s. Instead, I study Christmas. In doing so there were many surprises to come across. Allow me to share a few with you.

Did you know at one time the celebration of Christmas was once actually outlawed here in the America? It's true. It is one of the points which creates the most astonishment during interviews and podcast appearances. It's not the most contentious though. Early Puritan settlers in the original colonies felt any form of celebration was unnecessary and distracted from religious discipline. Yet it was deemed a worthy day off from work for many. As many men will do when given the gift of extra time off labor they decided to drink and Christmas day in the colonies became a problem. Not only for religious leaders but for law enforcement as well. Domestic arguments increased as did petty theft and vandalism. By the year 1659 leaders in Boston had had enough and all Christmas observances were banned by law. Anyone caught celebrating was arrested and fined two shillings. The ban was revoked twenty-two years later in 1681 by Massachusetts governor, Edmund Andros. (Prohibition in America and the 18th amendment outlawing of the sale of alcohol lasted 13 years from 1920 to 1933. The ban on Christmas lasted nine years longer.) The lyrics of the classic Christmas carol, "We Wish You a Merry Christmas," refers to bringing out your figgy pudding and a demand to bring it right here! The song is mocking law enforcement. Police would walk the streets on Christmas Eve shouting those words because one of the primary ingredients of figgy pudding is rum and a sure indication you were celebrating the holiday. One of our favorite Christmas carols was actually an early police protest song.

My next comment is made purely out of food for thought and not out of judgment in any way, but it was those who thought themselves as the most devout Christians in early America who banned the holiday. They were not alone. Twelve years earlier English parliament had done the same thing which included Ireland, Wales, and Scotland. They even banned any celebrations of Easter as well, with fines levied for anyone who did not comply. Does it mean current day Christians should push to ban all holiday festivities? I certainly hope not and those who tout the holiday as having become too secular or commercialized are devaluing the vast list of positives which come from such. I will touch on this a little later so keep on reading.

We all tend to think of Christmas as having always been a constant and time-honored celebration. It fills us with nostalgia and warm memories of innocence and childhood, but all things change throughout time. We think of our American traditions as being everlasting but most of the things we hold dear to our hearts at Christmas time are relatively new. It wasn't until the 1820's people here started to embrace the holiday as one to truly celebrate. To most Americans before then it was a simple day of religious remembrance and not much more. The practice of bringing a tree into one's home at Christmas time had origi-nated in Germany almost two hundred years earlier but it took until the 1830's before we did it. The image of Santa Clause did not even exist in the minds of Americans until the Civil war and even then, his image was conjured up as northern propaganda. Yet if were to I asked you right now, as an adult, to close your eyes and think of him, the face which comes to mind is exactly the same as it is for every kid in North America. It is part of the beauty of Santa Clause. Rarely is the perspective of both adults and children seen through the same set of eyes. I like to think it means there is still a kid in each and every one of us. Especially at Christmas time. Although the man in red's appearance is a far cry from the historical figure he is based upon.

Saint Nicholas was a Christian bishop who lived in Asia Minor during the early forth century A.D. He was most likely very thin as he tended to give away all his worldly possessions to those who needed them more. In those days in what is now modern-day Turkey few people were fat and jolly unless they had power and wealth. Yet even with the bishop's generosity I still like to think of Santa as one who might benefit from laying off the cookies. The first images of Santa here in America were created by a Bavarian immigrant and Civil War political cartoonist, and he had done so as Union propaganda. His name was Thomas Nast. They appeared on January 3, 1863, as a series of drawings in Harpers Weekly with Santa being shown handing out gifts to union troops in an army camp. He was not yet wearing a red suit but rather a jacket with union stars and pants colored in red and white stripes. Thomas Nast also went on to create the iconic symbols of both the Republican and Democratic parties with the donkey and the elephant. He would go on to draw Santa several more times throughout his career sometimes with a red coat and sometimes in green but give him credit for the cap and suit with the fur lining and big belt buckle. It wasn't until 1931 the Coca-Cola company brilliantly decided to use Santa in marketing campaigns and the commercialism of Christmas truly began. They hired an illustrator by the name of Haddon Sundblom to create an image for their advertisements during the holidays and it was he who forever dressed him in red and white. (Coca-Cola colors by the way.) He fattened up the guy a bit and put a big smile on his face and rosy cheeks and it is what most of us now think of when conjuring up what Santa might look like. A far cry from a skinny moderately dark-skinned dude from the middle east whose generosity and kindness were the factual foundation for the whole story to begin with.

As children we are regaled with stories of our Christmas hero as if he has been with us since time immemorial yet he has only existed as we imagine him for less than a hundred years. At the time of this writing my father is ninety-six years of age. It was in his generation that Santa Claus became the jolly man we all know and love. Does that surprise you?

Sundblom created new paintings each year for Coca-Cola between 1931-1964. One year he absentmindedly forgot to paint a wedding ring on Santa's finger and thousands of fans wrote letters to Coca-Cola in Atlanta asking what happened to Mrs. Claus. When Sundblom wasn't making his living doing commercial work he painted or drew sexy renditions of beautiful women and Hollywood starlets which became known as, "pin-up girls," to our soldiers during World War II. The soldiers coveted the calendars he drew and pinned them to their bunks as a reminder of home. Can you imagine the wholesome Santa smoking cigarettes today? He did. Before the ban on selling cigarettes on TV was passed in 1971 Santa could be seen puffing on Marlboros, Pall Malls, Camels, and many other brands.

Listen, we have all been manipulated and indoctrinated a bit at Christmas time. So much of what we know and celebrate this time of year was manufactured to either sell us something or persuade our way of thinking. Our entire childhood memories of what Santa Clause looks like was created to sell soft drinks! Christmas is the most persuasive time of year and those who persuade are well aware of it. The holidays are the most profitable time of the year, and most retailers build their entire financial year around it. Millions of people work full time and year-round in the Christmas industry. It puts food on the table for their families and spurs our economy and let's face it, we enjoy it. Christmas makes people happy so is that wrong?

The definition of irony is me telling you such in a book I wrote about Christmas and then sold to you at Christmas time. Right?

Would you be surprised to know in different countries they portray the image of Father Christmas differently? In the Netherlands they still refer to him as St. Nicholas, but his image is based on an old Teutonic god named Woden a.k.a., Odin. At Christmas time he rides through the night sky handing out presents from the back of an eight footed grey horse. In Britain they call him Father Christmas. Sinterklaas delivers gifts in Holland and Kris Kringle does the same in Germany. I know, I know, we as Americans don't like thinking whatever we hold as our traditions are less than the best and the thought of our Santa flying on the back of a horse with eight hooves seems almost laughable. Yet is it any different than a sleigh being pulled by flying reindeer? No, but it is what we have been told since youth. Plus, what does it matter if the message of kindness and giving is once again the same no matter where one happens to live? The spirit of Christian giving during the holidays is almost universal, well at least planetary.

Our American portrayal of Santa Claus is known by 7/8ths of all people on Earth and part of the reason is because Coca-Cola is now sold in every country worldwide with the exception of Cuba and North Korea. He has become not only a beverage spokesperson but also an ambassador of the American way of life. American television specials are translated and broadcast in almost every nation as well and those shows are enjoyed even by those who prefer to hang on to their own century old traditions of who hands out presents to children on Christmas.

We call him Santa Claus but in Russia it is Dedt Moroz. Papai Noel in Brazil. In Japan he is known as Hoteiosho and in Turkey Noel Baba. We leave milk and cookies out for him but in in England he is treated with a mince pie and a nip of sherry. Irish tradition is to leave out a pint of Guinness. In Italy a glass of wine and tangerines is the usual and perhaps in order to prevent driving a sleigh while under the influence and a possible D.U.I. charge they leave their gifts out on the night of December 5th instead of the 25th. In Russia they celebrate on January 7.

I find it interesting American traditions have very much influenced other countries during the holidays. In Japan it is now tradition to celebrate with a meal (and I am not kidding,) of Kentucky Fried Chicken and a special addition of Pepsi that tastes like strawberry cake. The one image of Christmas which very much started here in the United States which has circled the globe is the vision of majestic snow falls during this time of year. Yet half of our planet celebrates Christmas in the southern half of the equator during their summer season. Heck, even here few people who do not live in northern states rarely experience a white Christmas or ever dash through any snow. So, why is it the case? Simple, because Madison Avenue is located in NYC, and they write the ads and the songs.

Ask any child where Santa Claus lives and without having to think they will say the North Pole. Why is that? Because Thomas

Nast decided he did. He drew it in a series of sketches for Harpers Weekly published December 29, 1866, entitled, "Santa Claus and His Works," and above them was a banner which read *Santa Claussville, N.P.* and it stuck. N.P. North Pole, what else could it be? So, it was and so it is. It was forty-three years later before any human being had ever reached the polar ice caps and the first undisputed reaching of the North Pole. In 1926 Roald Amundsen, a Norwegian explorer was the expedition leader of a sixteen-man crew who flew a dirigible or blimp over the North Pole, but it counted. There had been other land attempts before that by Americans Frederick Cook in1908, and Robert Perry in1909, but later scrutinization of their claims through the years has cast enough doubt as to question their success. No one knows why Thomas Nast chose the North Pole as the basis of Santa's home base, but I like to think he did so because the North Pole was the one place on the globe which did not belong to anyone. Even today it is not a country. No artificial lines drawn on any map by men who wish to control something or someone. In fact, you will never see the North Pole itself on any map because The Artic is not a land mass but instead an ice flow in the Artic Ocean and therefore is always moving. I like to think the man who made his living by drawing political cartoons and propaganda kept his inner thoughts of what Santa should be as one who belonged to no one in particular and everyone in general.

I hate to admit it but so much of what we know as Christmas tradition and imagery has been based on an attempt at swaying someone's opinion in one way or another whether it be marketing or politics. Christmas did not even become a federal holiday in this country until June 26th, 1870, during the presidency of Ulysses S. Grant. (Who by the way makes for an interesting trivia question when asked what the S stands for in his middle name. The answer is nothing. It is simply the letter S and nothing more.) He had declared Christmas as a national holiday in hopes of reuniting the north and the south after the Civil War. So much of what we now think of Christmas traditions have their roots in persuasion throughout the years.

I do not tell you these truths to shatter any one's beliefs I only do so purely to point out the facts themselves have little bearing on keeping the magic of the holiday alive. Kindness is kindness. Does it really matter if the image of who a child might dream of on Christmas Eve might be different than that dreamed of in American beds? Let them dream. I am not here to correct anyone. In a world where disappointment is all too commonplace, I find a sense of peace in knowing on Christmas Eve people everywhere feel what I feel. I know reindeer can't really fly but I would still like to think they could on Christmas Eve.

Speaking of reindeer when you think of them what gender would you assume them to be? Go off of your memory of all you were told as a child. You might think singing the song Rudolph the Red-Nosed Reindeer in your head might help in your decision because it was the first time anyone named them in song. It was written by Johnny Marks who by the way was a Jewish songwriter specializing in writing Christmas songs. What? Yes. Does it matter, ... No.

The man wrote a great song which has been enjoyed by virtually every child while growing up and I would bet you lunch money right now you can recite every word of it regardless of your religious beliefs. If a man writing a song about an imaginary and fictitious reindeer with a light bulb for his nose now somehow offends you simply because you now know the back story, then it bears the question of whether you understand the true emotion of secular Christmas at all.

His brother-in-law Robert worked in the ad department of Montgomery Wards Department Store and had been taxed to write a color brochure in 1939 to be handed out to children during the holidays. It was he who created the printed story of the loner misfit reindeer who became a hero. Johnny liked the story so much he put it to music, and it became a No.1 hit sung by country legend Gene Autry in 1949. It wasn't his only famous holiday tune. He also wrote "Rockin' Around the Christmas Tree", which was a big hit for singer Brenda Lee, and "I Heard the Bells on Christmas Day" for Bing Crosby plus many more. When the animation special Rudolph the Red-Nosed Reindeer aired on NBC on December 6, 1964, it was Johnny who had written most of the musical score and the songs those of us my age still remembers. It is still my favorite Christmas show and I never miss it each year. Remembering every song lyric and all the dialogue.

In his song he listed the reindeer by name, Dasher and Dancer and Prancer and Vixen, Comet and Cupid, Donner and Blitzen. Before I get myself in trouble with anyone when talking about gender these days; I will leave it up to you to decide which might have been implied but here are the facts. Antlers. Yes Antlers. Reindeer are the only species of deer where the females as well as the males grow antlers. During the mating season which is referred to as, "the rut," males lose their antlers, and the rut ends in mid-December. Therefore, if the image we have of Santa's sleigh being pulled by eight tiny reindeer on

Christmas Eve includes those antlers, then we have to conclude rationally it was the females who did the work. Chalk one up for women's equality. I hope that story did not upset you. Talking facts about imaginary flying creatures. People tend to get upset when they find out what they believed in for so long might not be all we thought it to be. Isn't this time of year supposed to be about peace on Earth and good will towards all. Yet I have seen the dark side of people this time of year when old traditions are challenged.

When my former employer made the decision to strive to be more inclusive and add black Santas and elves to our product assortment there were some who expressed their outrage. Personally, I was outraged by their outrage. St. Nicholas was from Turkey after all. Knowing the facts should lesson divisiveness but sadly it is not always the case.

For the sake of discussion can we come to an agreement before I continue? There are many ways in which to celebrate Christmas and for the purpose of simplification would you allow me to separate them into two categories? The first is spiritually based and are determined by one's faith and personal beliefs and it is never my place or wish to question anyone's faith. The second category is those traditions of a secular basis and even though their origin might have had a religious connotation such as St. Nicholas being one who was truly sainted for his good deeds we don't think of Santa as a religious figure, right? I hope only to point out both with no judgment. Many of which started out with the purest of religious symbolism only to become secularized over the ages with people forgetting their original meanings.

It is said the first ever Christmas tree was created in Germany in 1536 by the religious reformer Martin Luther. The story is told of him walking through a pine forest late at night in late December near his home in Wittenberg. Looking up through the bows of a tree he saw brilliant stars lighting the clear and cold night sky. He thought of what the night sky must have looked like on the night of Jesus's birth with one star shining brighter than the others and decided to cut a small tree down and take it home. He placed candles in the branches and one at the top to remind his children to think of what Jesus might have seen with his own eyes. (The fact that pine trees did not grow in Bethlehem in those days makes no difference. Martin Luther never traveled to Jerusalem or surrounding areas, but I give the man the credit for his vision and devotion.) In Europe, the pine tree itself had long been revered during wintertime for over a thousand years as a sign of resilience for keeping its evergreen color when most others seemed to die off. Attis, an agricultural god worshiped in ancient Rome was celebrated during the winter solstice by people bringing into their homes his symbol, a pine tree. Europeans had been placing pine boughs in their homes during winter as a sign of new hope to come in the spring for centuries. So, the practice was not new. Martin Luther did not invent it. What he did do though, was lite it with candles and for that I give him credit. A lot of Christmas traditions are the morphing of earlier practices repurposed for Christian times.

His neighbors must have thought him to be off his rocker when seen dragging a flammable tree with pine tar and resin into his home then placing lit candles in the bows. I admire his faith. If one were to travel to Israel as I have you will see lots of pine trees today. After World War II, Israel was once again de-clared an independent country after two thousand years on May 14, 1948, and the Israeli government started importing pine trees from Europe. Many of which came from the same lands Martin Luther might have walked over four hundred years before. Pine trees thrive in dry land and the Jewish National Fund has since planted over 200 million trees of several species.

Ever since Thomas Edison came through with his viable electric light bulbs, many people have simply forgotten why we put trees in our home this time of year. It has become a Christmas habit more so than a symbol and we simply enjoy the light show and warm glow. By the way, it was Thomas Edison's business partner who invented Christmas lights not Thomas Edison as most people believe. Old Tom liked to take credit for anything invented in his shop even if it was not his idea. Tom was known for being kind of a jerk. His partner Edward Hibberd Johnson deserved the credit. He hand-wired 80 small bulbs in colors of red, white, and blue and strung them on a tree at the holiday. Today the Christmas lighting industry in America generates over seven billion dollars in sales and employs tens of thousands of people. Today artificial and plastic pre-lit trees are what most people buy, and it begs the question once again of does it matter? I don't think so as long as our emotions are genuine and not fabricated or manufactured.

Anyway, I mentioned two types of Christmases earlier because I do not wish to offend anyone with the history of the holiday, but I remember a case when I unintentionally did just that.

I once pointed out in an interview the reason we celebrate Christmas on December twenty fifth had nothing to do with the date of Jesus's birth. I should have thought better and left that fact out. As American's we love well told stories of our history even if they have no basis in fact or evidence. If I asked you who sewed the first American flag you would recite from memory and textbooks you read as a child; and proudly declare with absolute certainty the name of Betsy Ross. I'm sorry, but you would be wrong. I know, this analogy has nothing to do with Christmas, but it still makes my point. Time has a way of making us believe things are factual simply because it is what we have heard for so long. Years after Betsy Ross had passed away it was her grandson in Philadelphia who claimed it was his Nana who had done so. She was an upholsterer during her lifetime not a seamstress. She had done some alterations work for General George Washington who hired her in a pinch to mend continental soldiers' uniforms and sew on lost buttons and there are verifiable and documented receipts to show as such. Sadly, her work was so shoddy he refused to pay her, but the grandson's story stuck, and history books ran with it. We liked the story. It made us feel good to put a face on such an important symbol as our flag. On his death bed many years later, the grandson recanted his story, but no one cared. The story was a good one, so it was repeated. I live outside of Philadelphia and as much as this city is cloaked in wonderful stories of revolutionary pride it doesn't mean they are all true. Betsy Ross's house was the first woman's home in America declared a national historical sight and we even have a bridge named after her which spans the Delaware River. But to point out the truth and change the history books would only result in anger for many. Our Liberty Bell cracked the very first time they attempted to make it peel yet we treasure it as a national icon. Thankfully we can blame the British since it was cast in London in 1752 but, I am not sure another example of shoddy workmanship should be so highly prized as a symbol of American pride. Some people prefer a good story to the facts, I guess.

Anyway, back to Christmas. Just because we have been told something so many times does not make it the truth. When I mentioned Jesus was most likely never born on what we call Christmas day it caused an outroar. Doing so was not my intent. As an author and self proclaimed historian I simply pointed out what has been historically documented and I separated it from lore. My comment was not groundbreaking or even of my own for it had been recognized by theologians and biblical scholars for over a thousand years. The decision to celebrate Christ's birth on December 25th was dictated hundreds of years after the event and with absolutely no basis in any bible verse whatsoever.

Christmas became Christmas in the year 336 AD during the reign of emperor Constantine. Constantine was the first Roman Emperor to pledge his alliance and faith to the new religion of Christianity. In doing so he decreed the celebration of Jesus's birth would be in December as a way of appeasing those roman citizens who celebrated the pagan festival of the Winter Solstice. It was a month-long revelry of feasting and consumption superior to any college frat house toga party; only their togas were real and not bed sheets repurposed for the event. Much like in the early Massachusetts colony when drinking became a problem. So, Constantine simply changed the reason for the celebration without cancelling the party. He limited it to one week instead of a month and everyone was happy to see they still had something to look forward to each winter. Nowhere in the bible does it make any reference to the actual date or even time of year of Jesus's birth. In my mind it means any day on the calendar might be correct so keep the spirit alive all year long and not just between the dates of Thanksgiving and New Year's. Biblical scholars have speculated over the centuries on his actual birth date or at least the season and although I am certainly no member of academia, I have my own opinions.

There is a reference in the bible of shepherds sleeping in the fields at night to tend their sheep at the time of Jesus's birth (Luke 2:8) and it would only have been the case during late spring or the summer not the winter. Joseph and Mary had been making the trek from Nazareth where they lived to the town of Bethlehem to be counted in the Roman census. It was a Roman decree each subject of Rome must do so every fourteen years and it was required a man also do so in the town in which he had been born and Joseph had been born in Bethlehem. There is also talk of them returning to Bethlehem to pay taxes but as we all know it doesn't matter where you live the tax collectors will find you. It makes sense. Considering Mary was pregnant, and the trip is ninety miles it must have taken many days if not weeks.

The Gospels describe Joseph as a "tekton," which means a carpenter so he was a man of blue color means and there were few places for one to stay overnight on the journey so it must be assumed they slept under the stars. Any loving husband would wish to make the trip easier on his wife when the weather was warmer at night and less chance of rain or cold. Especially in her condition. It rarely rains in the middle east during the summer. My mentioning the lack of biblical verse substantiating December 25th as the true date of Jesus's birth caused an uproar. People don't like having what they believe being challenged. Even if my intent was to spread a message of Christmas cheer all year long.

I told the story during an interview back in 2015 and the backlash was truly surprising. The outrage it created was not unlike the villagers grabbing their pitchforks and torches while demanding to storm the castle gates. I got hate mail. Lots of it. I received threats of violence towards myself and my family by those who declared their Christian faith in capital letters and venom. I even had ministers and clergy who threatened me. It frightened me. It also made me question a lot of things. I decided to bow out of interviews for two years. Part of my own thoughts of the innocence of the holiday were lost for a while.

Chapter 10

Unrecognized Miracles

When I was little, I prayed to Santa. I even wrote him letters. Back then like today my prayers are always conversations with a friend not just requests. They were times when I could ask questions into the air hoping they might be answered someday. I also prayed to God, but I never thought to write him a letter. I just always figured God was busy with bigger matters and respected his time, but I always thought Santa would be listening. I never confused the two and never thought of Santa as a religious figure or divinity. In the mind of a child, I just thought of Santa as a force for good and if he could make reindeer fly, he must have been granted such powers by one even more powerful than himself. I figured Santa Claus and God were close friends and buddies. I loved both equally when I was a child and never wished to disappoint either one. Santa had his list of who was naughty and nice, and I figured God did so as well. As an adult I know one was purely fictitious but there have been times in my life when I wondered if the second might be as well. As a kid those questions are difficult to ask, and they don't grow any easier simply through age or time spent.

Either by God's divine plan, which to be honest with my childhood challenges, I always wondered how I might fit in. Or because of the kindness of people around me I have often times been blessed beyond expectations. Christmas and New Year's come very close together and the connection has never been lost to me. New Years is a time of reset and a new start. It's not just the flipping of a page on a calendar. To a student it is also the end of a semester and another chance. I have tremendous respect for teachers and in fact I married one. With such said it was not a blanket statement for I have dealt with more than a few who have devastated me at chalk boards with little patience and even less understanding. Those are faces and names I have long put behind me. There were those however who have greatly impacted and shaped my life by looking way past textbooks and taking the time and compassion to install confidence in one few ever expected to succeed. There are Santa's here on earth. If you are more comfortable calling them angels, I will not disagree. Allow me to share two stories if I might.

In ninth grade my Earth Science teacher Mr. Lee threw us a pop quiz with ten questions on it. One of them was to define the term *nodule*. I had studied but had somehow missed this piece of information and had absolutely no clue as to what the correct answer was. Falling back on my only playground defense of avoiding harassment I went with comedy and wrote down the answer: "Nodule Comaneci was a world-famous gymnast in the 1976 Olympics." The right answer from the Merriam-Webster dictionary defines a nodule as a small mass of rounded or irregular shape: such as a small, rounded lump of a mineral or mineral aggregate. By the way, I typed the quote from the dictionary from memory and without having to look it up almost fifty years later. Now I admit it wasn't my best joke and was one of those times where you had to be there moments, but it was the best I could come up with on short notice. Nadia (not nodule,) Comaneci was a Romanian gymnast in the recent Summer Olympics and became a worldwide celebrity and media darling. At age 14 she had become the first gymnast to receive a perfect 10.0 score. She went on to be awarded six more perfect scores and won three gold medals in Montreal that year.

I knew the answer was nowhere near correct but sometimes you have to go for it anyway. Mr. Lee sat down to grade the papers while we watched a short film and from the darkness of the room and towards the front, I heard him laugh. His laughter was not sarcastic it was genuine, and I knew I had been the one to provide it. I don't know that I can explain the feeling I only knew it felt good. He had seen me making classmates giggle with silliness before class but other than my parents I had never made any adult laugh out loud. Just before the end of class he passed back our papers. I had eight of the questions correct which was good enough for a "B," but he had written a note at the top in red pen. I usually hated red pen. He had circled my joke and wrote, "very funny." He even drew a smiley face. My score was an A. The joke had earned me extra credit.

He asked me if I wouldn't mind reading my answer to question six out loud and share it with the class. He prefaced his request by saying I didn't have to if I wished not to. In class in those days, you stood to speak whenever asked. I did and the class laughed when I read the question and then my answer aloud. The laughter was genuine and different. I knew what it was to be laughed at and had suffered it many times before but on this occasion, it was earned as a reward for thinking differently than others and amusing them. Everyone in 1976 knew who Nadia Comaneci was and the laughter was short lived, but it was powerful. "Well done, Dan...That was the wrongest answer to any quiz question I have ever given out, but your answer was funny and that counts for something." Mr. Lee's comment garnered additional laughs but, there was no sense of admonishment whatsoever in his tone of voice or the smile on his face. In every profession you will find those who feel they don't just have a job, but a calling and Mr. Lee was such an educator. He asked me if I wanted additional extra credit and an opportunity to turn that "A" into an "A+"? "Go home and look up the right answer and come back tomorrow with five more funny examples of what a nodule is, and I will let you read them before class."

I do not remember all five jokes, but I remember one. Again, a nodule is a small mass of rounded or irregular shape. A lump. The joke was, "what do you call a lazy nodule? ... A bump on a log." It was my first comedy audience and I enjoyed hearing laughter which was not directed at me but with me. Later Mr. Lee would task me to write something funny about other science terms or even riff on topic on demand while covering a subject. My answers were not always as funny as I might have hoped but he was forcing me to think. He challenged me to exercise my brain in a way no one else had ever done and science became my favorite subject. His style was never taught in textbooks. Textbooks were simply a tool for learning, but he taught by compassion. I will never forget what a nodule is.

In September of 2006 I made a few phone calls to my old middle school and was able to track down his home phone number. The woman who answered the phone had told me emphatically teacher's phone numbers are never given out. I politely asked again explaining he had been my 9th grade teacher and I simply wished to speak to him if at all possible after all these years. She reiterated the school policy but then paused. She then requested I repeat my name and I did. "Wait, are you the Dan Hughes who is on QVC?"

"Yes, ma'am I am, and it is why I was calling." I am always somewhat surprised and taken aback if someone recognizes me because there will always be far more people who do not than there ever will who do. "I would really like to call Mr. Lee and thank him for the confidence he gave me all those years ago." Before she broke the forbidden rule, she went on to tell me in great detail every piece of jewelry she had ever purchased, why she had done so and how much she enjoyed the show. She asked me not to tell where I had gotten his number but passed it along anyway.

My primary purpose was indeed to thank the man. I did though have a secondary agenda. I had always been taught there were nine planets in our solar system. It had been in my textbooks my entire life. And much like the internet textbooks never lie, right? In August of 2006 astronomers determined that Pluto was no longer to be classified as a planet. Like so many companies and employees over the years poor Pluto had been downsized to what is now referred to as a dwarf planet. Sad really after all those years. Pluto had played in the big leagues for years after being the last one to be discovered and was then deemed unworthy and sent back down to the minor leagues. A crushing blow to the ego of a planet who already knew he would never have the makings of a star. My earlier textbooks had been wrong. Imagine that?

On a different quiz and at Mr. Lee's request to list the planets in order. I had forgotten Pluto completely and left it off the list. In astronomical terms Pluto had been the last one picked to play dodge ball in gym class and for that reason alone I should have empathized and at least remembered his presence but had not. Neptune our eighth planet had been recognized as fully worthy 84 years before anyone even knew of Pluto's existence but then it is always easier to spot the gas giants in the heavens much like it is here on Earth. In 1930 Pluto was discovered and got his chance at the big time and must have enjoyed joining the team and eating lunch at the cool kid's table. Pluto was the smallest planet in the solar system. Our own moon is almost one-third larger. Yet, for seventy-six years he must have felt proud even though he was the last one picked to just be part of the team. Pluto had finally been accepted as an equal and it wasn't a bad run. The small guy doesn't hope for more than to be recognized as one who belongs but there is always the fear one day you will be called out for your shortcomings and asked to leave once again. The coldness and loneliness of deep space has been felt by more than a few right here on Earth.

Apparently even with my educational challenges I was a man before my time, and I jokingly told Mr. Lee I wanted either a higher test score on a 30-year-old exam for omitting Pluto from the list or at the very least a public retraction. We spoke on the phone for over two hours. Mr. Lee was then in his late 70's and I was pleasantly surprised he had indeed remembered me as a student but has also followed my work. When I say my work, I did not mean QVC.

After high school I knew college was not in the cards, so I moved to San Francisco and started doing stand-up comedy. At first, I had to work other jobs to pay my rent. I dressed up like Big Bird for children's birthday parties, cleaned hospital bathrooms and repaired and sold ceiling fans for a retail chain. At night I did open mics and corporate gigs six nights a week. San Francisco was a hot bed for comics back then and the hottest club was The Punchline on Battery Street. My only dream at the time was to one day work there. It was the home club for Robin Williams and many other greats, but the unspoken rule was you never performed there until you were ready. Getting booed there or bombing was my nightmare of nightmares, and I was in the audience every week on their open mic nights to see many do just that. There were a lot of comedians or at least those who hoped to become one whose dreams were dashed and ended with one bad set. I felt their pain perhaps more than others and continued to write and perform in much lesser valued venues until I thought I might just perhaps be ready. It took me a long time to muster up the courage for my first open mic night there. I wrote jokes while scrubbing toilets on my knees. My cockroach infested apartment while always scrubbed clean with my germaphobia was always still littered with yellow note pads scribbled with thoughts, observations and one-liner's. The night I finally made the decision to sign my name on the open call sheet for eight minutes on stage it just so happened Robin Williams was also there. Much like the night of the one performance of Gary Microwave and the Leftovers back home I threw up twice in the bathroom before going on stage.

You do a lot of soul searching with your head in a commode, and I almost walked out, left California, and returned to Indiana. Instead, I thought back to 9th grade and Mr. Lee. Standing in front of his class with a stupid joke about a nodule. The laughter I received in his classroom back then was addictive. Reinforcing and accepting and as shallow as it may sound it felt like love. Wiping the spit from my chin was not bravery it was desperation and a thought of what else can I do to continue to feel the same.

Robin Williams was a force of nature and king of San Francisco comedy. He would pop in at The Punchline unannounced to work on new material and the audience never knew when he might show up. I was on stage when he stepped out of the shadows at the back of the room and the audience erupted in applause. Comedy clubs are dark and not well lit with the exception of the stage and from my vantage point I couldn't see much. The timing was such I had just told my best joke on a set I had worked on for several months. I had gotten the laugh I had hoped for, but it was two seconds later the applause for him shook the building. There are rules in comedy and unspoken etiquette. I had seen several younger and unpolished comedians such as myself relinquish the stage when Robin walked in as a show of respect but, I apparently was the only one in the room who did not know he was there. Also, I did not know he had stood in the back in the shadows for five minutes into my eight-minute set listening.

Someone in the back had turned around and saw him at the doorway and started the applause. Instead of hanging up the mic as was the proper thing to do and make way for a genius I continued my set as he walked to the stage. When I saw him in the lights I simply said, purely as a joke, "Oh, my first night here and I thought I was killing it. That's embarrassing... I almost took a bow! Turns out the biggest applause I ever got wasn't even for me!" The comment was not said in any anger it was simply self-effacing and my usual style. I did go on to add, "Wow, comedy is the only profession that once you make it people give you a standing ovation even before you do anything. They don't do that for doctors, Robin. No one applauds in the operating room before they perform surgery."

I had managed to pull a few more laughs for myself before he took the stage and the biggest came from him. Instead of doing the proper thing I just decided to be the MC and introduce him. It wasn't my job to do so. Most comics just stopped midsentence and walked off. There is actually a thing where one needs no introduction. Instead, I said, "Ladies and gentlemen you are about to witness comedy genius! You also just saw the crushing of a young man's dream from the Midwest who thought your love was meant for him." I got one last laugh and even applause which were my own and waved Robin on stage, and he hugged me. At the same time, he whispered in my ear, "That was funny! Hang around and we will talk after my set." And we did. He performed for over an hour, and I have never laughed so hard. He did not have an entourage. Like myself he had arrived by himself and afterwards we sat late into the early morning hours in the green room just talking. He took my set and punched it up, gave me advice and as intimidated as I was to have met my first big celebrity he was never condescending. He asked questions and took the time to really listen to answers.

He had a way of making you forget he was a celebrity or a star when talking with him; yet there was always a sense of a mask he did not want others to see through. It was almost as if he felt he needed to always be funny so as not to disappoint what others expected of him. I had been at QVC for twenty-five years when like most people I heard of his demise at his own hands on the news. As an adult I do not cry often but I did then. My brain could not comprehend how someone so special, so talented could come to such a decision. We were not close. I don't pretend to have been in his inner circle. Much like the many celebrities I worked with while at QVC over the years there is a blessing in even knowing them on a professional level and there have been more than a few who touched me with their kindness. There were other occasions when we might run into each other, but I was not one to initiate contact. He was in a stratosphere and orbit I was not able to understand. The early morning after my first open mic night at The Punchline in San Francisco I left the club at around 3:30 AM and took a cab back to my apartment feeling like somehow something in my life had changed but not understanding what it was. The same morning at 9:00 AM I got a phone call from a club owner I did not know and had never met. It was a club in the bay area I had never worked in or even been too, but the owner had called to book me for the next weekend as an opening act. It paid two-hundred dollars a night but felt like a million. I asked him how he had even heard of me, and he simply said a friend had called earlier that morning and told him to book me. I didn't ask who. I didn't need to. I was very sincere when saying goodnight to Robin on the night in which we met. Thanking him for his kindness to a new comedian and a scared kid from Indiana. In hindsight I wished I had yelled my thanks for everyone to hear. I really do not think he had any idea of how much he impacted others with his humor and his compassion. His passing was a message to many: the thought that you must have it all or it is nothing, never brings true happiness.

I have had the honor and pleasure of doing stand-up over the last forty years with the likes of many much better than myself at the craft. I had opened for Joan Rivers years before she came to QVC to sell jewelry and we became personal friends. I have also had the pleasure of doing stand-up with Jay Leno who I also feel close to and Indianapolis native David Letterman. Few people will ever remember me as a comic, and I am fine with that. It more than paid the bills in those early days, and it was a lot more fun than scrubbing toilets. For seven and a half years I made my living on stage before coming to QVC, telling stories with punchlines, making people laugh. From one who was once afraid to stand in front of a classroom I had found a niche I fit into against many odds. I never became famous in comedy or even in TV, but you don't have to be the biggest dog to still eat well.

Every year during Memorial Day weekend I would book at least one show back in Indiana at Crackers in my hometown of Indianapolis. It is the same time as the running of the Indianapolis 500 and a sacred time for those of us who call ourselves Hoosiers. It was on those occasions I met and worked with David Letterman a few years before he moved from NBC and Late Night with David Letterman to CBS for twenty more plus years as host of The Late Show. Mr. Lee told me he had been to several of those performances. I asked Mr. Lee why he had not come up and said hello and he told me he didn't think I would remember him from so many years ago. He was wrong. As nice as it was to meet David Letterman and work beside him, I would have been even more excited to have greeted and hugged the man who gave me a chance to be me as I am without judgment or check marks. After working on the same comedy billing with David Letterman in Indy a few times David passed me a business card and told me to call him. I never did. David has always been very kind and even gracious but the thought and fear of failure on national TV if given the chance was enough to prevent me from picking up the phone. I don't live my life thinking too much about regrets, but I do still wonder what might be different had I been brave enough to have made that call. Instead, I focus on the blessings which have become reality and my thankfulness for just being where I am today.

Twenty years ago, I bought a small farm here in Pennsylvania for my new bride and we have raised cattle and sheep and have horses. She adores animals and I adore her. The farm reminds me of my Indiana roots and with my responsibilities with being on air at QVC the place keeps me busy and humble. It is difficult to think of yourself as important or better than others when you have sheep shit on your shoes before going to work at your day job. Even when the day job is on national TV. Our place is called Punchline Farms in honor of those earlier days in San Francisco. I take tremendous pride in past accomplishments, but I will never forget I did not do it alone. I thank Mr. Lee for my first few moments of stage time in a classroom in Indiana and even though I never made it as a household name or Hollywood celebrity I am content. Too often I have seen how such fame becomes painful and the epitome of the phrase, "Be careful what you ask for."

*   *   *   *

The second story I will call Christmas Fruit. He was my English Literature and Grammar teacher from my sophomore year until graduation and he flunked me two years in a row. When fellow students enjoyed the summer sun, I was back in school two hours a day five days a week. Can you name the one teacher in your lifetime who impacted your future more so than any other? I can. His name was David Fruits. That man yelled at me more than any other teacher I had ever had. He was relentless and I thank him. Again, there have never been participation trophies in my life. He should have flunked me and I deserved it as well. Without excuses I had not measured up to the work. His yelling was measured at me most often when I thought to give up and he would not allow me to do so. He was the first teacher who swore in my presence. He treated me as an adult, and he had volunteered his two hours a day five days a week two summers in a row. "Damn it Danny you're smart! This stuff is not beyond you. You have a tremendous memory, and we can figure it out together. You will probably never need algebra in your future, but you will need English skills and I am not giving up on you until you get this. Forget about the letters themselves. Grammar is nothing more than remembering the rules. Use your memory."

David Fruits was one of my first teachers who took a true interest in understanding the dyslexic mind. His passion was literature, and you can't have literature without proper grammar. He understood the power of the spoken word and reveled even more in the permanence of those words when written on paper. My reading skills back then were subpar but not far from average national scores. All the help my mother had given me earlier in life had helped me to compensate but I still had issues with comprehension. People like me find it difficult to multi-task. Focusing on a scrambled letter in my mind would often make me forget what I had just read seconds beforehand.

The average reading speed is between 200 and 250 words per minute with a comprehension and memory of just 60%. He taught me the letters in a word really do not matter and not to focus on each one as if it were a mathematical equation of the first letter plus the second and then the third added up to the word itself. The flash cards I had studied in my youth had allowed me to recognize complete words without needing to read them letter by letter. He took that lesson to the next level. He told me to focus on only the first and last letters of a word and then reference it mentally with my memory of the dictionary my mother had made me memorize. I didn't need to count letters in between consciously. I could look at a word and if the first and last letter of the word were correct, I could usually figure out what was in between with a glance instead of true focus. Letters are letters but words represent things, and I was good with visuals. In the first summer of working with him between my sophomore and junior year my reading rate increased from 160 words per minute to 230. The next school year with even more help to 335 words per minute with comprehension level of almost 90%. For some reason I can read and remember entire paragraphs word for word. What will slow me down even to this day is not trusting myself so I will re-read something twice or even three times until I am confident enough to commit to knowing the subject matter without doubt. Reading out loud is a different beast altogether. When reading silently if one makes a mistake no one knows but you. If a letter or number is jumbled, I can work it out in time by the relationship of that letter within the context of the others around it. Numbers are not so easy. When taxed to read aloud mistakes are easily recognized and therefore my pace slows to what feels like a crawl. As an adult even today reading aloud is stressful.

He also pushed me in a direction I had not considered before and one I was not truly comfortable in. He recommended I join the high school radio program and even though I was at first very nervous, there was a certain comfort in knowing it was in a booth by myself hiding behind a microphone. It was almost like talking to myself which I did often, and the microphone was like a shield, which allowed me to create a radio persona much more confident than I truly was. The thought of public speaking in front of any size crowd other than one or two classmates was still terrifying. He told me if I joined his speech and debate team for the next year, he would pass me through my sophomore year. "You have great verbal skills, and you are a good story-teller. Let's develop those talents. They will take you farther than you might imagine." He forced me to push myself in areas he saw strengths in I had not yet seen for myself. While math teachers simply gave me a D for the year and passed me to the next year's teacher to deal with, he held me accountable. Again, I thank him. Over the next two years I competed in original oratory and debate and surprising to me I often won. He was not surprised at all.

I credit him with my high school diploma. My last semester of senior year was the first and only time I ever made the honor roll. I was and always will be uncomfortable with public speaking even with so many years having done so. The Guinness book of World Records officially lists Regis Philbin with holding the accolade of the most hours hosting national television with just over 17,000 hours in his 52-year career. Before that was Hugh Downs who held the record with a total count of 15,188 hours. At the time of this writing, I have surpassed both in my 33 years at QVC and did so without cue cards, teleprompters, scripts, or a producer who can yell, "Cut, let's do it again." My last count was over 19,000 hours and I was working towards 20,000 when in March of 2023 my days at QVC came to an end while told by management it was a cost cutting measure and no reflection on my performance. QVC is live TV except for a few overnight hours which are tape repeats of earlier shifts. For many years we operated as true live twenty-four hours a day. Whereas most shows on television are thirty or sixty minutes in length the average daily shift for a host on QVC is three or four hours; so, the amount of time racks up over the years.

Televised Shopping has never garnered much credit for the impact it makes on peoples' lives and sadly no one working in our genre of TV has ever been awarded an Emmy Award for their hard work. I do not mean just the host but also producers, lighting and sound engineers, set designers and technical directors. Yet even though there is a category listed as, "Reality Television," our genre has been completely ignored as noteworthy or impactful. What is more realistic than when an inventor who worked so hard to create, develop, and manufacture something of their creation and then seeing it become a national success and reaping the financial rewards which changes his or her family future for the better? I thought that was the American dream after all. I was given the opportunity to be an influential cog in that most important wheel, and I am proud of having been so.

None of it would have been possible had Mr. Fruits not had faith in me. Or the fact he took the time out of his own schedule to mentor and support. I do joke with friends it would be nice one day to have my name and star on Hollywood's Walk of Fame, but I would be even happier if it was cast in cement behind Grauman's Chinese Theatre and closer to the dumpster instead of the sidewalk out front. It might be inspiration to a younger version of me somewhere who never craved the limelight but still dreamed of success.

I told Mr. Fruits in my senior year I was thinking about becoming a lawyer and he called me out. "You are not cut out to be a lawyer Dan. You'll never make it!"

"But I have done well in debate, and you told me I could do anything I put my mind to. Besides lawyers make good money."

"Yes, you are, and yes, I did but you're still not cut out to be an attorney. They will eat you alive. You do not deal well with confrontation and probably never will. You can change your destiny, but you can't change who you are. Lawyers are wolves and you are a rabbit. It's not an insult Dan it is just who you are. You like to help people and make others happy. You like to entertain and make them laugh. I don't think you would be happy as a lawyer even if it paid you well. You do realize you will most likely always have to work harder than others to get the same results, right?"

I knew exactly what he meant. He had mirrored the same words my mother had often told me, but he did not know it at the time. "If you are going to work that hard, he went on to say, it might as well be something which makes you happy too." So, after high school I took a few different jobs in retail and even tried a corporate position for a while but then took a chance and packed up and moved to San Francisco. I had not seen or spoken to Mr. Fruits in forty years since graduation. If there is one thing, I can say in defense of social media, it does afford people the opportunity to reconnect. At the same time, it can also be a vicious cesspool inhabited by those who spout opinions while hiding from behind keyboards the way I hid behind a microphone. There is a difference though. Mr. Fruits was correct; I am a rabbit. I have never felt joy in hurting anyone along the way and have always tried very hard to choose my words carefully. He reached out to me on Facebook with a friend request in December of 2019 and I was more than happy to accept. Through Instant Messenger we exchanged phone numbers and set an appointment to talk on my next night off. We wound up talking for over four hours.

He peppered me with questions mostly about the celebrities who have appeared on QVC and what working with each might have been like. What he was most curious about was who was the most difficult to work with and I told him. And no, I won't repeat what I said. Sadly, there have been more than a few. There have also been those who were tremendously gracious over the years and those who have become lifelong friends. I also told him of my proudest moments which were those of working with inventors and helping them to be successful while bringing their ideas and products to a national television audience. I often reminded him of his part in the equation, but he humbly dismissed it and asked for more stories. He did tell me he had retired twenty years earlier and moved to Finland with his life partner of many years which came to me as a surprise. He had moved because of what he felt was intolerance and prejudice in this country and it made me sad he had felt the need to do so. Perhaps I was naïve, but I knew nothing of his proclivity, nor did it matter. I did think back to whispers in the hallways and huddled jokes, and I am sure his last name of Fruits was most often the punchline. I even mentioned it although not as a punchline of my own. He chuckled though and said, "Yeah, labels suck, don't they," and I knew what he meant. The word retard is not socially acceptable now days, but I had heard it more times than I wish to count in my earliest days.

At the end of our long conversation, I asked him a question. After once again thanking him for his mentorship and confidence in me I asked how he came to find me on Facebook since he lived in Helsinki and QVC America only broadcasts here. QVC has sister networks doing what I did in London, Germany, Japan, Italy, and China but their programming is separate from one another. He told me he was on YouTube one night and saw a video of QVC bloopers and although I look much different from my high school years, he told me he recognized my laugh. His comment alone made me laugh again. I figured early onset baldness in my thirties was God's way of keeping me humble and I never thought my laugh was distinctive in any way. Yet he remembered it. He also told me he was proud of my accomplishments. I once again reminded him of his impact, and we said goodnight. Just before doing so, he mentioned his husband was also on Facebook and told me I should send a friend request to him as he had many more photos on his link than he had taken himself and I did. I had only known him as an amazing teacher, and I wanted to know more about him than just the role of an educator. It has often been difficult for me to step out of those roles I learned when much younger but, on that evening, he had said, "Call me David. You're not a kid anymore." I had never thought of any teacher as a friend, but he became one during that call. I again thanked him and in closing he said, "No Dan. I thank you. You have no idea what this call has meant to me."

I do not know if his words were in hopes of confirmation of a job well done or an affirmation of having done so. Either way we tend to forget those who we always think of as so strong are still human beings. Thank you goes a long way. He never mentioned stage four pancreatic cancer. He never brought it up. His Husband instant messaged me between Christmas and New Years of that year to tell me he had passed. I still call Jari on the date of his passing, and we talk for a bit. He is most happy when I tell him stories of how David would yell at me, and his response is always the same. "Yeah, that sounds like him. God, I miss him." Jari is now in his mid-80's but has never been in another relationship. He is content in keeping the memory alive of someone he loved. I felt sadness in losing a mentor and one I had just had the opportunity to span a distance of forty years, but I could never fathom Jari's pain. He told me on the second year we talked he had set up a tree to remember Christmases past with David. He had sighed before saying so then chuckled, "David would have liked that." Even from four thousand miles away I could tell he was smiling. I honestly don't know if I could be as strong if forced to ponder the anguish of losing the woman I adore.

All of us who are blessed to live long enough will have memories of those we appreciate but are no longer with us at the holidays. Some are friends, some are even more so and of course there is also family to remember as well. At first it is never easy and even more painful when that first Christmas rolls around. I lost my own Christmas spirit for a few years after my mother passed away. I think it is normal and all of us who have suffered such losses tend to balance grief with happiness as a measuring stick. As if finding anything to smile about at Christmas somehow equals a failure to be sad at the same time. Isn't sadness how we prove to ourselves how much we loved those individuals? Jari was a psychologist before he retired, and I probably got more free advice during our once-a-year phone calls then those in Hollywood pay a fortune for. He told me David would not have wished him to be unhappy during the holidays. Much like his love while they were together was predicated on happiness so would Jari's future. By choice.

I am sure there is at least a few of you who are reading this who might have recently lost a loved one. Allow me to say my heart goes out to you. This time of year, more so than others our emotions run deep. Allow them to do so. Good and bad. But choose to remember the best of them and the things you shared with the ones you lost from previous Christmases which made you smile and laugh; and then repeat them. Do not dismiss those memories as if they no longer matter. Embrace them as even more important than before. Relive those times as if the one you lost were still with you and they will return. I know, it's not the same but just like when we were children with the anticipation of good things to come, choosing to celebrate the good times can still bring smiles and dial down the pain. Think of how much your loved one would have appreciated the tradition and knowing it had continued even after they were no longer with us. This keeps their memory alive. Don't let the joy fade. Loved ones lost do not wish us pain and I do not believe they wish us to suffer after they have left us just to prove their own importance while you were together.

I often hear people at this time of year say they simply do not feel the holiday spirit as if it is something which must be bestowed upon us. I don't think it works that way. Instead, I truly believe it is something we must look for within ourselves. Even when things have not gone the way we would have liked. Without any promises made I know this advice can make a difference. In the U.S. Declaration of Independence there are three beautifully written and wise assurances made. Our forefathers referred to them as unalienable rights and they are as follows: Life, liberty, and the pursuit of happiness. Happiness itself is not a guarantee or an entitlement promised to anyone; it must be pursued. It must be a goal we work towards and there are times when the path is difficult. It begins with a covenant we make with ourselves to seek it out and if we are vigilant enough and continue to believe, it is still there to rediscover once again. Believing in happiness is not the same as childhood faith in flying reindeer at Christmas time. For all of us when we were young, we were eventually taught it was silly to still believe in things we should have outgrown but maybe again it is just another part of the magic of this time of year. The silliness of secular Christmas is the joy to a child. If becoming an adult means believing only what is true in the here and now, then you're missing out on the whole package, and I don't mean a gift-wrapped package under a tree. We grow up and become adults with bills and responsibilities but there is always a part of each one of us who remembers being the kid who believed. It doesn't leave us. It never leaves us. Dreamers when young are told to grow up. I know a lot of successful people these days who ignored the demand of acting their age or becoming a realist and prospered and found happiness by doing so. Allow yourself to think like the child you once were during the holidays. Trust me, for I know it works.

Dreaming of the impossible or even the irrational still opens our minds to possibilities the stoics tend never to see. Ask any inventor with a new idea. Any artist, composer or successful entrepreneur didn't get there by listening to the naysayers and they didn't overcome the odds, they simply ignored them. If becoming an adult means forgetting how to play and have fun then even at my age, I am not in any hurry to do so. Christmas is the best time to remember what it was like when we were children and enjoy the moment. Remember to make time for happiness. Remember to remember.

Chapter 11

The Night the Animals Talked.

It was a parable, a legend, a fable, a tale. So went the first words sung in the children's Christmas animated special 'The Night the Animals Talked'. It first appeared on December 9th, 1970, on ABC and was a joint production between American and Italian Television and based on an old Norwegian holiday story of the interaction of the animals in the stables in which Jesus had been born. Forgive the historian in me but when most of us think of Jesus as having been born in a manger, but it is not true. Now before you too grab your pitchforks and torches for another trip towards the castle allow me to explain. A manger is either a feeding trough or a container for water not the barn or stable itself. Yet somehow, we have come to think of the entire surroundings as a manger. Knowing otherwise does not diminish the humble roots of the story of his birth in any way. I own a farm and have several what you might call mangers on the property to feed livestock, but no one refers to them as such today. In the days of Jesus, they would have been stone blocks hand hollowed out for the purpose, but today they tend to be galvanized steel or plastic multi-manufactured on assembly lines instead of rough-hewn from stone.

Nowhere in the Bible is there any reference to Jesus being born in a manger it is just what people think today. There is though scripture (Luke 2:4-7,) that when Mary gave birth to Jesus, "She wrapped him in cloths and laid him in a manger, because there was no room for them in the inn." I know, it is a matter of pure semantics, but I look for truths. Looking for them does not mean a diminished faith. I would rather have all the facts before making important decisions and not simply go on what I might have been told over the years. If one truly wishes to study the bible then semantics and ancient history play a big part in understanding.

This may surprise you but there is also no single scripture in the Bible which places Jesus' birth in a barn or a stable either. It is a logical assumption formulated by people hundreds or even thousands of years after the blessed event and mention of the manger makes for a logical connection to such. I know it challenges most of our common thoughts. Is it possible nativity scenes we all know and love at Christmas time and a major part of our religious decorations might have it off by just a bit?

Archaeologically speaking in ancient Israel and Palestine few people had separate wooden structures in which to house livestock. Wood was at a premium. The average citizen lived in a modest two story dwelling made of clay bricks and the first floor was designated for housing precious livestock. Especially during inclement weather. Those with even less money housed their animals in a cave hewn out of the side of a cliff and built their brick home alongside. It is why in the year 330AD Emperor Constantine built the Church of the Nativity over a series of caves in Bethlehem. Constantine was Roman not Jewish and never set foot in Jerusalem but he sent his mother Helena there after being the first Roman leader to officially recognize Christianity as a legal religion. Historians and scholars still debate on whether he had done so for his own religious beliefs or as a politician who simply wanted to lessen public unrest. Either way his Mother, who had no archeological training whatso ever, returned to Rome in 328AD with remarkable finds. One of which were pieces of the true cross Jesus had been crucified along with nails in which he had been impaled. Miraculously she also discovered the very cave he had been interred, as well as the one he was thought to have been born in. Amazing really considering for over three hundred years biblical scholars and historians had been looking for the same to no avail. The Emperor claimed them to be true and who is going to argue with the Emperor? Helena would later be sainted by The Roman Catholic Church.

The telling word in Luke's scripture is his mention of there being no room in the *inn*. It is a modern translation of the ancient Hebrew word *katalyman* which means a place of lodging or guest room usually designated for family or close associates. It did not mean a hotel or space to rent. Even the term guest room is misleading since most had little space but willingly gave up their own place of rest to one who was welcomed in. I believe Jesus was born on the first level of a home usually reserved for livestock.

Joseph may have known or even been related to the owner of the house in which he and Mary stayed on the night of Jesus' birth. The fact the inn had been filled makes sense since Emperor Augustus had demanded a worldwide census of all Roman subjects in order to obtain taxes. Everyone born in Bethlehem as Joseph was needed to return home in order to pay their tax and be counted. There must have been a lot of crowed homes during the census. Humility and a desire for privacy during Mary's most delicate time makes sense for Joseph to have thankfully excepted the bottom floor in their time of need. In the Jewish religion hospitality is practiced as a demand of God yet Jesus being born where livestock is held might have been a simple matter of Mary not being able to climb a flight of stairs or ascend a ladder when Jesus decided to make his appearance.

I do not pretend to know the world's most importance answers to the most important questions but I have spent over forty years constantly asking the question of why. It has never about debunking current thoughts it has simply been a personal quest for understanding.

Allow me to take you back in time and put you in the setting of the most important night in human history. Much of what we think of as the idealized version of Christmas night has been sanitized and disinfected with thoughts of fresh straw and three wise men standing nearby wearing fancy robes with gold brocade in attendance, but both are most certainly not the case. As far as the setting goes anyone who owns livestock knows the truth. Even though I tend to be a neat freak and crave order and cleanliness in my life I know stalls of any kind at nighttime become filthy. What shepherds, herdsman and farmers refer to as mud is rarely made up of just dirt and water alone. Unless Joseph and Mary had prayed that sheep could not poop for the night, (Which would have been a miracle in and of itself. Believe me I know.) I am betting the location Mary and Joseph bedded down in that night were much like my own stalls. We have all seen pristine nativity settings outside of churches and even in our homes during the holidays which are referred to as crèches and it is a word borrowed from the French only referring to the manger itself. I would bet few of our holiday decorations today would include the squalor they endured.

The surroundings of Jesus' birth are even more humbling than most nowadays would expect. Never in a Christmas setting does one see piles of dung or the imagery of what a stall really smells like. Thinking of the reality of that night for many somehow diminishes the importance of Jesus' birth. Yet remember no one fully understood the full significance of the two weary travelers and one on the way who had entered Bethlehem on that evening. To me it only reinforces his most humble beginnings. All of us tend to think of the past filtered by what we have been told and comparing that to what is currently thought of, but therein lies the importance of faith. Faith does not mean blind following or fellowship. It simply means taking the time to read between the lines without prejudice of preconceived ideas and allowing the meaning of a two-thousand-year-old story to come to life in your mind and heart while accepting some of what might have been told and taught is not correct. If history books written in much shorter spans of time have gotten things incorrect, then I do not fault people's interpretations of biblical scripture to be any different after so many millennia. If my comment offended, it was certainly not my intent in which to do so.

The King James Bible or as it has come to be known as The Holy Bible was completed and published in 1611. Over sixteen hundred years after the blessed night in Bethlehem. Yet it is the "Official Bible of England," and the only bible of the English church. There is an earlier version dating from 600 years previously called the Leningrad Codex which is a standardized version of earlier Hebrew text but few people other than biblical scholars or geeks like me have heard of it. King James was most assuredly aware of its scripture but chose to ignore most of it when deciding what was truth and what was not. There are currently over 40 versions of the New Testament in print here in our country and the Bible has been translated in over 2000 languages over the years. I say so only as a reference point and not as inflammatory or a bone of contention to anyone's beliefs or religious practices but purely as a way of asking you as you read; to put yourself in the sandals of Joseph and Mary on that night. Imagine what they were feeling. Doing so makes the setting more personal and impactful.

There were no wise men or magi, or as we all now sing in a popular Christmas tune of "We Three Kings of Orient Are," who attended the humble beginnings. In the gospel of Matthew in chapter two he mentioned wise men without numbering them and never referred to them as magi or kings and he never mentioned them being there at the time of Jesus' birth. In fact, Matthew was the only one to bring up the topic of wise men at all. Luke made no mention of them in his writings. We tend to think of them as kings by the expensive gifts they came bearing but it is most likely not the case. Kings do not travel in small groups then or now. The number three was most likely settled on by thinking of the three gifts mentioned of gold, frankincense, and myrrh and the title of those strangers elevated to Kingship most likely came from the Christmas carol written by American clergyman John Henry Hopkins Jr. in 1857 with the lyrics, "We three kings of Orient are, bearing gifts, we traverse a far," (most of us sing it by saying travel a far instead of traverse but no one likes a nitpicker.) Anyway, you know the song so back to the story.

In Mathew's description of the wise men making their visit it is written in scripture: "And when they came into the house, they saw the young child with Mary his mother, and fell down and worshipped him." It is written in the very same chapter as his description of the blessed night but not specifically written as such. We tend in our minds to compress time as if it was a spectacular event everyone should have recognized in the moment. Young child, not infant or baby. House not stable or barn. The point I am making is that if and when those wise men arrived it was not on the night of his birth but several weeks, months or even years later. No one knows for sure how long Mary and Joseph stayed in Bethlehem but according to Jewish tradition and law it was at least forty days. According to the Gospel of Luke, Mary and Joseph left Bethlehem forty days after having arrived, which would have been in accordance with Jewish tradition and the amount of time required for the "purification," of the mother. The word after does not designate a definitive length of time. Had the three wise men been there on the night of Jesus' birth it would have conflicted with the humility of the moment and diminished the message would it not?

There was no one there to herald in his beginning. No kings, no wise men in fancy robes and certainly no little drummer boy. Even a God-fearing woman such as Mary would have strangled a kid who walked into the setting with a snare drum if her new-born child had finally just fallen asleep, and after going through the pains of childbirth. We have sanitized that night in our minds because we now know of its importance but back then it was still yet to be discovered. With the possible exception of a mid-wife Mary and Joseph were very much alone except for the animals there. It was as it was supposed to be. They must have been tired and scared, and I believe it was only those animals in the stable who were the ones blessed to witness the event. If only they could talk.

Mary had traveled many miles on either the back of a don-key or on foot. The trek from Nazareth to Bethlehem is roughly 90 miles. Average walking pace is somewhere between two and a half and four miles per hour so the journey most likely took four days if they walked eight hours a day. All while pregnant and uncomfortable. I don't think as a husband myself that Jo-seph would had begun the journey without a preplanned des-tination in which to stay when they arrived in Bethlehem. Espe-cially with Mary in such a condition.

We tend to think of Mary and Joseph as having to beg in order to find a place to stay but I do not believe it to be the case. Joseph was a carpenter and must have been a good one. At the days of the end of the Old Testament and the beginning of the new, Hebrew law was strict and strongly enforced. It was the days of, "an eye for an eye." If a carpenter built a structure or house which fell on the one who paid for it, then a family member of the carpenter could be put to death as repentance as equal justice. Jesus' parents were not poor, but they were not wealthy either. They were certainly not beggars but only those cast into a position of feeling they had no choice but to acquiesce to what space was available. Remember, it is easier for a poor man to feel humble for having nothing than it is a man with something to have to settle for less.

The term, "middle class,' is an American description and was only coined in the 1830's and before then there were either wealthy landowners or pretty much everyone else. For Joseph to take an extended stay away from work he must have counted on his reputation with confidence to offset his lost wages and spendings in which to provide for his growing family in the future. The coins in his pocket were not enough to secure an upper room or inn simply because the inn or top floor was already full. Plus, thinking your coins make you entitled is the definition of arrogance and Joseph was not an arrogant man.

Mary and Joseph were no vagabonds they were simply those who could not compete with a no vacancy sign. A good man who works with his hands tends to take pride in not only his work but also in his ability to provide for family and bedding down with livestock must have been tough while wondering if he had failed his wife in her time of need. Jesus having been born in a stall was not only the humblest of roots to the newborn baby it was also that of his parents.

Seeing his son born in such conditions and his wife having to do so must have been difficult. Joseph had already felt the shame of wedding a pregnant woman who was carrying a child he knew was not his own. She had become so out of wedlock and before the marriage and her apparent unfaithfulness came with strict repercussions. Joseph was a devout man and followed the law and his first reaction was to break the engagement which was logical in the situation, but he decided not to bring more shame upon her by publicly calling her out. He must have loved her very much. Plus, under Jewish law he could have had her put to death by stoning in the public square. Imagine your own reaction if having to deal with his dilemma? Your loved one comes to you with a story of becoming pregnant not by another man but by God himself. As much as I adore my wife, I cannot imagine all of what went through his mind. When the Lord sent an angel to Joseph to confirm her story and to tell him it was God's will to marry her; Joseph readily accepted his faith and took her as his wife. He did so knowing he would be ridiculed but he did not care. He did so for his love of the woman and his faith in his creator.

As a writer and historian, I attempt as best I can to put myself in other peoples' shoes or in this case sandals at the time of the event. I also find in doing so it also personalizes history as a reflection on how we might all respond in that moment instead of just rhetoric and storytelling. I know the joy of being a first-time father. The fear of seeing his wife in so much pain yet the adulation of witnessing the miracle of birth and being overwhelmed with emotion. If I were quizzed on the paint color of the walls of the maternity ward it would be another failing grade. I do not remember the name of our physician back then or the name of any nurses. I just remember the feelings and they will never be forgotten. Joseph must also have been caught up in the moment and the stench and the filth were also forgotten. He had a son. His wife although tired was healthy. In such surroundings there must have been much happiness and thankfulness and I do believe the place in which he was born, whether it be the first floor of someone else's home, or barn, or stall, or stable, or cave, was filled with nothing but love. Perhaps that is the message after all. Maybe, just maybe, there is a reason why no archaeologist or historian has yet to definitively locate the spot where Jesus was born. I don't think we are supposed to know all the answers. I think we are supposed to look for love anywhere we dwell.

*　　*　　*　　*

My mother and I sat and watched the first airing of, 'The Night the Animals Talked' on ABC, and even as simplified as the animation was at that time compared to modern day computer graphics and technical effects, I was transfixed by the story. Since that night I have watched it dozens of times and although it is no longer broadcasted on TV you can find the original on YouTube and I recommend you watch it. Many of the most significant messages the producers were hoping to impress upon us were lost on me as a child and I took it as literal in meaning. The story was about the different animals in the barn yard and hierarchies which tend to dictate status and one's roll in life. Each was different from one another and much like cows moo and dogs bark each class of animal spoke different languages with little understanding of the other. The ox was the leader and the bully. The dog was the guardian. The sheep were, well sheep and the pigs were the lowest rung on the social ladder. None got along until that special night when two weary and tired travelers appeared in their barn yard and a star appeared in the east. Perhaps a miracle nearly as important as the birth, the animals were given the gift to communicate with each other for the first time.

A lot of our holiday specials have been written with social undertones and much can be read into them when looking for them, but I was simply fascinated by the thought the animals could talk. At first, they argued with each other trying to determine who was the most important and pointed their fingers, (or hooves,) at the ones they thought lesser of. There was jealousy and ego until they came to the realization of not wishing to act like people. When a lone donkey arrived at the door of the stable telling the others that he was traveling with a man and woman who would soon be giving birth he was turned away because none were willing to share their small patch of hay. It is a short animated special lasting only 24 minutes allowing an extra five and one half for commercial breaks. The producers packed a lot into those few minutes. Jealousy, status, ego, rivalry, opinion, all were mentioned and acted out by the animals in the barn until the ox sang a song entitled, "Let's Not Behave Like Humans." The animals recanted and Mary and Joseph were welcomed into the barn for the most important night in history. Even the pigs were allowed into the barn for the very first time to witness the miracle. I thought the pigs were cute and it made me happy they were not excluded and were accepted as equals by the others out of kindness for once.

The miracle of speech only lasted for that first Christmas Eve but in the moment, everyone got along no matter what their differences in heritage or their language barriers. It is a powerful story, and one mankind seems to easily forget. The next morning when the animals felt the need to spread the message of kindness with all in Bethlehem their ability to communicate went away and the ox who was the last to be able to speak was left to ponder if humanity would ever fully understand the miracle which had been bestowed upon us all. It is a good message but not what I had taken away while sitting next to mom on the sofa watching TV.

Animals could talk on Christmas Eve! Everyone got along and loved each other. Even the lowly pigs who had always been the outcasts were welcomed friends on the night before Christmas. I went upstairs and gathered up every stuffed animal I owned and borrowed those from my two sisters' room and put them out on my bedroom floor in a circle so they could all see each other when the magical time arrived. I knew stuffed animals were inanimate objects, but realists can still be dreamers, can't they? I was ten at the time.

I urge you to not only relive and celebrate whatever family tradition you have at this time of year, but to look to create new ones for the future. It wasn't until we moved here to the farm, I remembered the show from so many years before. It struck me as a pleasant coincidence that now we had barn stalls and a stable on our property. Sure, there were differences between the never disclosed birthplace of Jesus and no history book or even the bible has ever confirmed an exact location and of course my humble farm is thousands of miles and continents away from that place, but it still allowed me to have a better frame of reference as to what it might have been like. The smells in the air as an example.

Out of our five senses it is the ability to smell which is most closely linked to memory. Most likely it stems back to a time when prehistoric man was a gatherer of food and not a hunter. He would sniff a berry or plant before eating it and if he found himself sick later, would remember not to eat the same thing when smelling it again. My mother's fondness for roses always reminds me of her when I smell one. Like most people here in our country I tend to think of Christmas much more after the thoughts of summer have passed us and it begins to grow colder here in the northeast. I still think of Christmas as a time with the potential for snow even though I am aware it rarely snows in the middle east. I also no longer think of Christmas as just December either. Fresh cut summer hay has an aroma hard to describe to those who have never experienced it, but it is sweet and earthy and wonderful. When our barn had been completed and our menagerie began to grow, I was off-loading a wagon full of hay and found myself inhaling deeply and it triggered a thought. If Jesus might have been born during warmer months. Then perhaps tonight was the actual date, or tomorrow, or maybe the next. The Christmas spirit washed over me in June, and I walked to our barn and sat down in the straw and allowed my sense of smell to take me there to Bethlehem over two thousand years before. I took in the aroma of manure and woody fragrance of pine shavings and thought back to what it must have been like that night in Bethlehem.

I don't usually sit in a barn stall when there are chores to be done but it was a wonderful moment of contemplation. Kelly and I were raising cattle and sheep back then and it was before we owned horses like today, but I had bought a miniature mule at a livestock auction to save it from the butcher. I had never owned a mule and was a neophyte to farm ownership. I had never considered someone might sedate a troublesome animal before passing them off to another at a livestock sale. I named her Candace because of her sweet disposition at the time and how easily she was loaded into our livestock trailer. I only paid two hundred dollars for her, and it felt like a victory. I had saved her from a certain doom and wondered why no one else had bid on her much. There was little competition in the bidding and mostly it was just bidding up the new guy which was me. I have come to know after a few years a livestock auction is a lot like poker and there is as much bluffing as there is true interest. Bidding up the newcomer seems to be a game no one had informed me about. I probably paid twice what she was worth, and the local farmers most likely knew why. My wife had noticed each time I had raised my hand a few would laugh but I was too intent on saving the mule and never saw it.

By the time her sedatives wore off, (the mule, not my wife,) I had learned to call her by several other names and none of them were as sweet. Once we got her home she bucked and kicked at any attempt towards getting close to her. Other than the several dozen attempts at getting a rope around her we made little physical contact with her at all. Our humble farm is more of a petting zoo or animal sanctuary than an agricultural operation. We didn't need a mule. I wasn't looking for miniature labor to pull a tiny plow to till the back forty. Plus, our place is not that big, and we don't have a back forty. I just wanted her to settle in and feel the love both my wife and I have for animals. All I wanted in return was to give her an occasional ear rub and maybe a bit of reciprocation for the obvious kindness we had offered her. She also cribbed, which is a term I was not aware of, but it is when equine chew on wood either out of boredom or just plain meanness. She literally ate barn siding and most of her well-appointed stall and I had spent countless hours and weeks trying to calm her without avail.

I had no idea what Candace had been through before coming to our farm, but she tried my patience every day. The same morning, I had told my wife Candace had to go was the same day I had sat down in her stall to contemplate the night of Jesus' birth and just think for a bit, when Candace did something she had never done before. I had again spent weeks in hopes of bonding with her while even taking a lawn chair to the barn with a book just for her to get more comfortable with my presence. My mind was not on her it was on my thoughts as she came from our back field and stood at the entrance to her stall and just stood there. The more I ignored her the more inquisitive she became, and she came in and laid down within arm's reach of me. I let her sit for a while and took a chance and was finally able to reach out and stroke her neck and rub her head. The moment did not last long before she got up and walked back out to the pasture, but for those few moments it was love. It was Christmas, in June, in a barn setting much like most people think of from those earliest days in Bethlehem.

Every year on Christmas Eve just before midnight my wife knows I will disappear for a bit. I put on my favorite beige Carhartt jacket which is now faded and well-worn with a tattered red corduroy trim at the neckline and step out into the cold with a bucket. Inside are apples and carrots for the horses we now have, and sweet grain for the sheep. Each year at Christmas Kelly asks me if I want a new jacket and I always tell her no thank you. I like the one I have. Candace is no longer with us. We had no idea how old she was when I found her that day at auction and perhaps it was those more sophisticated in farming back then who laughed at one willing to bid on a stubborn mule whose time would soon be counted. She was only with us that first summer and I hope her earlier skittish life became better than before for being with us and the compassion we had to offer. Getting to the point where I could feed her by hand while rubbing her huge ears probably made me happier than her. Her stubbornness taught me patience I rarely possessed as a younger man, and she will never be forgotten. Neither will the memory of Christmas in June that first year after building the barn here. I have learned more about empathy in a barn yard than what most teachers ever taught me in a classroom with certain exceptions of course.

I am an adult now and no longer the same ten-year-old boy who thought just maybe the animals could indeed talk on Christmas Eve. But who am I to say what miracles happen at this time of year. I would rather just hedge my bet with kindness just in case. Our horses get their noses rubbed a bit longer than normal then on a regular day and each sheep eats an unexpected treat from the palm of my hand and it makes me feel content. We no longer raise cattle for it turns out I am not much of a farmer after all. Farming seems like a contradiction if you tell someone you love animals, but it is not. I had made the mistake of naming our first few head of Black Angus and when it came time to take them to market it made it difficult to do so. I still did though because farmers grow food and people are hungry. I do not fault stronger farmers than myself for doing what they need to do when their own family relies on the paycheck. We no longer claim farm status on income taxes and have not quoted income from here for a while. After losing Candace I made the decision to add a miniature donkey to the brood and then another so the first would have a playmate and Hershey and Dinky were added to the number of mouths we feed each day. They are two of the sweetest animals I have ever known and a welcome addition to our place.

On Christmas Eve I spend thirty minutes or so just enjoying the quiet making sure there is fresh straw in each stall and once again feeling like I am closer to those things which really matter. It is a special time to treasure. My stalls will never be fit for a king but perhaps, just perhaps with a little effort I can make them better than those Jesus' mother endured during her delicate time. I will check my watch, so I do not disturb the midnight hour and then in the stillness of the night and after the grain and apples have been consumed; I walk back to our farmhouse with the same phrase spoken from over my shoulder and out loud just in case, "Enjoy your conversation. I will see you in the morning. Merry Christmas!"

Chapter 12

Christmas Illumination

My fascination with Christmas lights cannot be explained. It is just one of those things you either understand or labels you as crazy or obsessed. There is no twelve-watt program for those of us addicted to them and to be honest I am not looking for a cure. For just a moment let's look purely at common sense and logic. Anyone who stands on a two-story ladder long after sunset and, in the cold, to string up one more strand of lights with numb fingers and a fear of heights must have certainly lost their mind. As it was in most cases it was my father who showed me the joy of lighting with perfection. Our house when growing up always had a few more lights than the neighbors and what he excelled in was making sure they were placed with great care and always in straight lines. Even taking the time to spray paint the wires between bulbs so they matched the color of our white gutters and thereby looked like they hung there magically in the air. We had a large plywood Santa on the side of the house he had cut out and painted himself and it is still in our family. It must be almost 70 years old at the time of this writing.

He would tell Mom he put up those lights to make the kids in the neighborhood happy, but he once confessed to me that Christmas lighting was a competitive sport, and he was not one who liked to lose. And he was right, on both counts. Perhaps there is a bit of ego involved in the process but there is also a pureness of heart to put out a display which pleases others as well. When my older brother had grown old enough to have outside interests other than standing in the cold to assist the master in his craft I was willingly drafted to the role. I took to the role much like Luke Skywalker sitting at the feet of Yoda and soaked in everything he taught of the art of exterior illumination. Dad would cut store bought lights and re-splice them, so each strand was custom fit to each gutter run. He preached what he called the rule of thirds where he always had lights up high on the top story, then those on the first floor and a third on the ground outlining our mulch beds and the garden in front of the porch. Those he called, "ground effects" and were mounted into metal stakes he made in the garage and were fabricated so each bulb would be at equal height of six inches off the ground.

My father was a purest and preferred the old C-7 glass bulbs to anything modern. He hated icicle lights which came out in 1996 saying they never hung straight and looked sloppy. The thought of LED's today would most likely make a vein on his forehead protrude. He was the consummate judge of other neighbors' work. Each year on Christmas Eve when we were young, he would load us kids into the back of our Plymouth station wagon. While we were dressed in pajamas and winter coats, and he and my mom would drive throughout the city as my father pointed out the shortcomings of our neighbors' Christmas spirit. He was in his glory, and I think it was his favorite part of the holidays. "Did they just throw them up there?" my father would comment out loud. "Cheese and rice, would you look at that!" Dad in his London Fog raincoat with a fedora on was in his element. As my older brother and sisters grew up the number of kids in the back seat thinned out but he had sucked me into his world of observation. It was a promotion of sorts for me.

Are you old enough to remember station wagons with the third-row bench seat which folded out of the storage area in the very back and always faced backwards and towards the tail gate? It was in the days long before mandatory seat belts. The youngest were always relegated to the farthest regions from the dashboard and I think I was eight years old before I realized highway signs had green paint and words printed on the front. From my view they were always just tin with no letters. Moving up to the back seat behind Mom and Dad was an opportunity to impress my father. I would stand in the back seat while resting my arms over the front seat, looking out the windows stating, "Dad, they should have put a few more lights on that bush. It looks like a twig."

"That's my boy!" Dad would say to Mom proudly. A chip off the old block."

I had but one rule for my wife Kelly during the holidays and the dates between Thanksgiving and Christmas when first married twenty some years ago. She was not allowed to plug a hair dryer in or run the vacuum cleaner after dark. Doing so was sure to blow a fuse or trip a breaker with the number of lights I had up on the house and in the yard. When we moved here to the farm it was my own chance at sharing what I had learned. We don't live on an estate and there are no iron gates at the entrance, but it is still more than I could ever have anticipated in my youth. The original property was built in 1790 as a one room stone house and added on to several times over the centuries. Its floorplan is quirky, and we enjoy it. Most of the rooms have only seven-foot ceilings and as claustrophobic as it might sound. We find the space to be warm and cozy. The original exterior stone walls are now interior walls separating the old from the new and with hewn beams on several ceilings the place has charm and its own personality.

It had originally been a cattle and poultry farm and we have photos from the 1850's of massive chicken houses down by the creek. By the time Kelly and I bought the place in the early 2000's most of the acreage had been sold off by past residents to real estate developers much like I had seen back home in Indiana where I grew up. The ten acres we purchased and the fact it was the original homestead was enough to grandfather farm status to us even though it had not seen barns, fences, or livestock in almost eighty years.

It took us three years of working every night and weekends to turn the place into our own with modern amenities and pipes which did not leak and upgraded electrical which could handle my dream. Our kitchen is now modern and a tad bigger than the original after knocking out a few walls, but the floor in there is two-hundred-year-old barn siding I hand planed in the driveway the first summer we were here. I taught myself how to repoint stonework and I know every nail in the barn because I sweated my tail off to build it, along with the outbuildings which were needed for farm equipment and hay storage. In the process I made sure we had electrical runs adequate for Christmas lights, with outdoor electrical outlets installed for that very purpose.

The work would begin long before Halloween when it was still warm here in Eastern Pennsylvania. Christmas lights and electricity are all about mathematics and mathematics had never been my strong suit. Most household current comes into a home at 120 volts where it is then sent to a main electrical panel with breakers or fuses which limit the amount of power to any one given part of the house. Breakers are rated at either 15 or 20 amps and each act as a safeguard to make sure things do not overheat or a fire hazard is created. A 15-amp breaker can handle a top load of 1800 watts. 20-amp breakers are installed for things like your furnace and stove which draw much more voltage and can handle 2400 watts before tripping the circuit. If the average C-7 Christmas bulb draws 2 watts, then in theory you could plug just under 900 of them in with one circuit before reaching or surpassing the maximum load of 1800 watts before the breaker is tripped. It also means anything else plugged into the same circuit such as a hair dryer or even a small table lamp would surpass the load. It is why when we remodeled the old place, I paid to have an electrician upgrade our system to 20 amps. When we built the barn, we did the same thing and then ran electrical lines with outdoor outlets to our new fence lines which surrounded the barn and outbuildings.

It took almost two months to string our first Christmas strands that year and each one came on a thousand-foot spool with bulbs spaced a foot apart and each one custom cut and fit to gutters and fence line. Even my father was impressed, and it felt good. Between crazy enough friends and I and my wife we put up over a mile of lighting. My wife did not fully understand the insanity, but she enjoyed seeing me so happy and long days of work turned into pizza parties with laughter and beer. Each year the display grew with added ground effects and lighting effects and when we fenced off our main pasture which encompasses a little more than six acres it created a mathematical dilemma. I wanted lights on those fence runs but the only way to do it was to run additional designated electrical lines underground and additional breakers in the barn to carry the load and that was something my wife wanted nothing to do with.

I am not the boss here at the farm. I am just simply the tallest one living here and it counts for little. The thought of trenching up new pastureland we had spent three years clearing of brush and scrub trees and seeding to sustain livestock was enough for her to invoke her marital veto powers. "We just spent a fortune on fencing and you're not going to tear up my pasture just for Christmas lights! You have enough already Dan. The place looks nice at Christmas. Why do you always have to overdo it?"

Wait, what? You can't overdo Christmas! "You are not digging up my pasture!" she told me. And the boss had spoken. The gauntlet had been thrown and it was up to me to come up with the answer. The answer was math. Crap! In order to get lights to where I wanted them, I couldn't add more electricity, so I had to do what I have done all my life and that was to come up with a better solution.

The wattage of a C-7 incandescent bulb is 2 watts but having owned a Christmas lighting business for a few years I knew LED bulbs of the same size only drew .75 watts. I had sold the company the year before but called in a few favors from old friends and distributors and was the first person to use commercial quality LEDs on a private residence here in the Philadelphia area. Using the newer technology allowed much longer runs without the worry of popping fuses and we were able to run 3200 feet of lighting on one circuit (just over half a mile with another football field in length to spare.). Here is the math. An acre of land equals 43,560 square feet and assuming the acre is equal on all four sides and then taking the square root of the land it equates to 209 feet for each of the four fence runs on each side. 4 x 209 equals 835 feet. The problem was my pasture was six acres in size or six times larger. So, 835 x 6 = 5010 feet, which is almost a mile. (A mile is 5280 linier feet.)

LEDs were expensive back then. Only theme parks and large downtown lighting displays used them in those days. The decision to switch out all our lights to the new technology was one my loving wife did not quite understand but she has always been supportive. Especially when I sold my 1934 Ford pick-up truck which was my first ever collector vehicle and one I had taken years to restore myself, to pay for the upgrade, but I have no regrets.

The new fences got their lights and we had enough left over to even light the old oak tree in the front yard which stood over a hundred feet tall. Not without the help of a cherry picker lift I rented, though with my fear of heights it was the first time I wondered if my wife's doubts of my own sanity had long been correct. During the process Kelly had seen and helped in the stringing of lights but I had saved the lighting for a special event. Test runs were only conducted when she was inside. I wanted to surprise her.

After my masterpiece was completed, I decided to throw a large holiday party for friends and family, and it was scheduled for the Saturday before Thanksgiving. Fully aware of how peoples' schedules are busy during Christmas time I thought it would be nice to bring in the spirit a bit early without imposing on folks. I wanted to do a lighting ceremony of grand pageantry and while lying in bed two weeks before the scheduled party another thought popped into my head. It had taken ten minutes or so to run from each outlet and plug to illuminate the display and I had tried working with timers, but they were unpredictable and could not offer the split-second timing I had envisioned for a lighting ceremony. I wanted a bit more drama. The words my father had told me rang in my head. "Christmas lighting is a competitive sport and I hate to lose." So, I reached out to those much smarter than myself.

When you work for a national television network you meet brilliant engineers and I have the utmost respect for those who can do those things which I cannot. The kindness and generosity of those I approached with my idea still fills me with gratitude. I had asked if it was possible to build remote controls which would allow me to light each outlet with a touch of a button instead of running around and plugging things in. Television remote controls had been around for years, and I wondered if the technology could be harnessed for my intended purpose. I asked some of our engineers at work and was told by most the answer was no. TV remotes work on infrared light and only when the remote and the television are both in line of sight and only for a short distance. When hoping to light up ten acres it would not resolve the problem. One of the engineers interrupted and said, "True, but if we used radio waves instead of infrared it might work."

"What type of distances are you talking about?" another one asked. I answered guessing at the farthest point from where I had hoped to do the lighting ceremony. "I don't know, maybe a thousand feet."

"Can't be done," one of them said and it started an argument. One, I simply took a step backwards from and watched with amazement. Four of our engineers circled a table grabbing pencil and paper. Hunched over and scribbling math I will never understand I only interrupted them once and was quickly hushed as they put themselves to task. It was asked with a question which then became a challenge which then became a mission. Four of the sound and electrical engineers I had approached volunteered not only their time but their expertise to create from scratch an amazing system, which they put together in either their homes after regular working hours or in my garage. Sometimes they worked way past midnight on a tight timeline to help me to see my vision come to life. They dissected remote controls from garage door openers and took parts and pieces off the shelf and created new technology which had never been used for Christmas lights before. They built radio wave remotes all on separate frequencies and operated by battery, which we then fitted in a wooden console I had crafted the morning of the party in my garage workshop. There were twenty-three wireless receptors which were plugged into each outdoor receptacle and each strand of lights then plugged into them. Today you can walk into any big box store which sells paint and drywall, and you will find Christmas light remotes, but they did not exist back then. I wish I had thought to patent the idea. I had offered to pay each one of them for their time and efforts and all four of them refused, stating how excited they were to see if their joint efforts would work. We tested each individual remote, one at a time, but chose not to test the whole system until that night of the party. I consider their help as just another act of Christmas kindness.

On the night of the party and after a few cocktails between friends and hors d'oeuvres, (wow, I had to look that word up to know how to spell it correctly.) I had struggled with the English language so forget about speaking French. I convinced every-one to step out into the cold once again and ushered them to-wards the pond which is in the front of our place. Most seemed a tad bit confused but complied as I took my role as P.T. Barnum offering the greatest Christmas show on Earth. It was all show-manship and tongue in cheek, but I wanted to please and at the same time I was worried and anxious things might not work.

My best buddy Tim, who I met over thirty years ago when he moved into the house next door to my first home here in Pennsylvania was my biggest ally. It has always seemed that no matter how hairbrained one of my plans might have sounded he was always in for the adventure. Tim helped me on a cold day earlier in November, another act of kindness, to sit in a row-boat for over six hours as we placed small styrofoam rafts which we anchored to the bottom of the pond with rebar and fishing line. We both froze our butts off yet I don't remember him com-plaining. What I do remember was both of us needing a bit of help getting out of the rowboat with cramped legs and the af-tereffects of the bottle of Fireball Schnapps we had sipped in an effort to stay warm. There are few blessings in life as strong as that of old friends.

Two hours before the party he was there once again rowing himself out to the pond to place luminaria, which are paper bags with sand in the bottom and candles in them and set the candles alight. Those in attendance were happy to see 100 glowing candles bobbing in the pond thinking it was the culmination of what was to be offered to that year's Christmas spirit. I had lit wreaths in every window and a few more other lights, but no one expected what was coming. I had kept the lighting ceremony as a surprise to those who had not worked on the project.

With 120 people in attendance, I asked if I might say a Christmas prayer and in doing so thanked all of those who had helped me and there were many. Those who had volunteered their time or expertise. Others simply for their friendship and camaraderie over the years. I was emotional. Pushing the first button the barn lit up as if by magic, off to the left and in the distance. And those around me made sounds usually reserved for fireworks on the fourth of July. The next button lit up the garage which was in the opposite direction and those present had to turn their heads to see it. There were still twenty-one buttons to push. We had all walked to the pond in the shadow of darkness. Each step had been taken with caution due to the blackness of the night. At each subsequent push of a button the darkness evaporated the gloom, and our humble home became a Christmas wonderland. The stone walkway to the pond and the wooden bridge we crossed over the creek to get to the pond a few moments ago in darkness was lit up with ground effects and lights on the bridge and the oohs and aahs continued. Then it was the dormers on the third floor followed by the gutter runs on the second floor. Then the first-floor gutters outlining the house and then the fence which separates our house from the garage by almost fifty-yards, (it was built as a carriage house years before automobiles had ever been invented.) Our home is not large or a mansion in any sense but continuous lighting from one end of the property to the other made it appear much larger than it is. The same way Disney uses lights to impress, and the effect was greater than I could have imagined.

I paused with two buttons left. There was already enough light to fully illuminate the faces of everyone present and it was nice to see their smiles. Many of my friends had brought their children and the smiles on the adults' faces were equally as childlike as their sons and daughters. I held my finger in the air and slowly lowered it towards the control panel for what all must have thought was the grand finale and it would have been worthy of such. The one thing we had not had time to test was the half mile of light which had been strung on the majestic oak tree in the front yard. I had run out of extension cords, and it was a neighbor who had offered to run to The Home Depot in town to secure one just before the party had started. In the darkness he had crept through the yard and plugged it in and then walked it back to the only outdoor receptacle still available. When I saw his smiling face, I said another silent prayer and crossed my fingers and hit the button.

I will never know who planted that tree, but it must have been at least long before the Civil War. It is the centerpiece of our farm logo on stationery and business cards and although few might notice it on paper there was no way to ignore it that November night. With over three-thousand white lights shining and each bough lighting up the night sky it could not be ignored, and people applauded. Then they hugged and felt the holiday spirit in just the way I had hoped for in the moment. My engineer friends slapped high fives in triumph for their hard work and deserved to do so. They had pulled off something which had not been done before. Most thought of the oak tree as the grand finale but I still had one last button to push.

I waited till things had subsided and simply said, "We're not done." I had received my applause and more praise than I had thought possible and to be honest it did feel good, but I wanted no credit for the last button to be pushed. It was not mine to take or to ask for. "As great as this moment feels between family and friends let's not forget the true meaning of Christmas. Kelly, would you do the honors please?" My wife walked even closer, and I showed her which last button to hit, and she did. Perched thirty feet above our barn was a ten-foot diameter star on a brass pole, still unseen in darkness, when almost the whole property had been lit. When she pushed the button there was no applause just silence. Strong, magical silence. It lasted for a moment in the cold air while at the same time no one there that night felt the chill. All the other lights were ignored and forgotten exactly as they should have been. The silence was what was most felt in the moment and my little slice of heaven in Pennsylvania became Bethlehem itself.

Our property sits in a valley and butts right up against a highway which is much traveled and always busy. We all stood silently just looking out at what had taken months to create and focusing on the star. Everyone was just taking in the moment and enjoying the feeling. The silence was powerful and lasted for quite a while and we all felt it together. Then the noise started. It began as just one honk from the highway then another. The first trucker who chose to show his support with a long blast of an air horn brought additional cheers from our party and a cacophony of horns followed for another ten seconds. When the air had once again grown silent, I felt as if God's hand was on my shoulder with his approval. It was not a feeling of pride but much more the humility of feeling acceptance and knowing the work had said something in meaning greater than myself.

As we all walked back up what was now a well-lit stone path to the house for a few hours of Christmas celebration and what I thought was a grand finale was all upstaged by the power of upmanship and awe only our creator and mother nature can produce. As if on que it began to snow. It rarely snows here in Pennsylvania before Thanksgiving, and these were not your usual flurries although even that would have been impactful. I had either missed it in the forecast which as a farmer I doubt since I always check the weather several times a day. It began to snow huge flakes. The type large enough to see their shape while floating like little sheets of paper towards the ground. It was magical and I was not the only one to feel it in the moment. My grand finale had been surpassed by snowflakes, but it did not matter. I was pleased to bow to my creator and even felt a bit guilty I had attempted to rival his ability in creating awe. One of my usual and always sarcastic buddies said loudly enough for everyone to hear, "Damn Hughes, nice lights, but how much did you pay God for the special effects!" Everyone laughed but I was still too caught up in emotion to comment. Kelly who was walking by my side holding my hand hugged me and then kissed my neck as she whispered in my ear, "Now I understand why you do it. Thank you. It's amazing."

"I didn't do the snow part," I said to her as if it was an honest confession.

She laughed. "No, but I think you got your message across and maybe God was watching."

Chapter 13

Out Done Even With The Best of Intentions

Kelly and I threw our holiday party and lighting ceremony for ten years here at our farm and each year I worked hard to top the previous year. Friends and family would mark the date of the Saturday night before Thanksgiving on their calendars months in advance. One year we secured reindeer from the Philadelphia Zoo and borrowed an antique sleigh from a friend and Santa made his arrival a bit earlier than normal. If I waited to illuminate the big oak tree a whole section of the front yard remained in shadow, and it was in that spot we showcased a new display each year at the end of the light show. Another year we built a crèche scene complete with live animals from our farm. We had chickens and a few of our sheep and although Candace was gone Hershey and Dinky made their acting debuts. I included actors from our local high school playing the part of Mary and Joseph and also included three wise men. (A showman always gives the people what they want.) Music was piped in for Christmas tunes as well. The giant star from above the barn was moved that year to reside above the nativity scene as it should be. My wife each year would chastise me lovingly for attempting to outdo myself knowing how much effort and work went into each year's display. Each subsequent year took weeks in planning, then months in which to see it all come together. Within five years we had automated the lighting by using two designated computers built purposely for the event and again was a first for residential lighting.

I am older now and the cold affects my bones in ways a younger man would not understand. For over thirty years I have worked well north of fifty hours a week at my primary career plus the demands of daily farm work and usual chores. Kelly and I have always shared the daily chores simply because we both feel if we needed to hire someone then it was a sign we had too much. I have always worried about turning down additional work or opportunities simply because I never knew when it would all dry up. Working hard to get to a point of financial stability also comes with a cold fear that at any given day it could all just disappear, and that fear is greater than never having reached success at all. Few people in my younger days had any expectations of what my life might become and to be honest neither did I. So, turning down voice over work or rejecting a weekend comedy gig seemed almost sinful. Working at a hectic pace was my way of proving myself. To whom I am still not so sure.

Back then I was cohosting a Morning show which aired live from 7:00 to 9:00 AM Mondays through Friday with a wakeup call at 3:15 AM and then long hours of production meetings after the show. Often, I would travel on the weekends to per-form comedy and although it brought in extra money it meant leaving Kelly with the farm chores, but she never complained. My life has never been about money. Sure, it provides some creature comforts and offers one a sense of independence. It also allows you to make some decisions others may not have the luxury of making, but it always comes with a price tag. It is a price you pay without ever knowing the cost until you're there.

It has always been difficult for me to say no.

When asked to become involved in local civic activities I did so uncomfortably fully aware I was not smarter than others. For someone who will never feel they belong in the limelight it was uncomfortable but my abilities in public speaking raised much needed fund raiser monies for several very worthwhile causes. It felt good to make a difference but the amount of energy and stress to prepare speeches and the additional hours of dinner banquets and tuxedoes started to take their toll, when added to my schedule. I had my first heart attack in February of 2013.

I was told after the fact it was a congenital condition, but self-imposed stress didn't help my cause. It wasn't on my to-do list on that early cold February morning, and I had missed all the warning signs. Heartburn for three weeks before was pushed aside as usual stress when you think so many are count-ing on you each day. Shortness of breath was counted as the possible onset of a chest cold, and the exhaustion was just par for the course with the demands of a hard-earned lifestyle when the mindset was you always had to work hard to prove your worth. There was never any chest pain other than heart-burn. No cold sweats or palpitations. Strangely enough it was an article in Cosmopolitan Magazine which triggered the thought there might be an issue at hand.

I hate to reveal any secret pages in a man's playbook of life but there are a handful of things I know as fact. If any ladies are reading this, here is one you may not know. A man will read anything close at hand when sitting on the toilet. We cannot help ourselves. It is ingrained in our DNA and whether it be counted as an attempt at multi-tasking or just perhaps pure boredom there is not a man among us who has not read the warning label on the back of a shampoo bottle while sitting there. Now I have never put much stock in Cosmo Magazine and any previous interactions with the information therein has never been to my benefit. In my younger days and during my first marriage I only knew if my first wife met me at the door after a long day of work with a Cosmo in one hand and a pen in the other, she had just taken a quiz and I was a jerk. None of the countless articles entitled, "How to Get a Man," or "How to Keep a Man," or "Twenty Things to Do to Please Him," were ever read as tutorials in marital bliss but the quiz in the back was always read as irrefutable documented fact and deserving of wrath. It is much like the thought process of your spouse having dreamt you committed a vial and despicable act and when awakening they are actually mad at you in real life because if they could have dreamt it, you most certainly must be capable of it. I have apologized not only for things I have never done but also for things I wasn't even aware I was apologizing for.

The article was entitled "4 Heart Attack Symptoms Women Should Never Ignore." In it was mentioned jaw pain. Jaw pain? Strangely enough when the chronic heartburn awoke me at 2:00 AM it was accompanied with what I thought was a tooth ache just below one of my rear molars. It had not been there when I went to bed and with my infallible male logic, I said to myself, "Self, you work on TV and wear makeup for a living. Maybe you should go get this checked out!" The decision saved my life. I will no longer mock Cosmo Magazine and even may one day think those quizzes are written purely to make me a better man. Okay maybe not, but anyway.

There was some guilt when awaking my wife at 2:15 AM and saying, "I don't want to worry you, but something doesn't feel right." We happen to live within five miles from a hospital and I told her, "This heartburn is not going away, and I just want to get it checked out, okay." She knows I am somewhat germophobic by nature and like many farmers I don't tend to go to the doctor unless something is either bleeding, broken or falling off. Even then I might need to be yelled at before going. I am no macho man, but I have stitched myself up a few times here at home. Volunteering to go to the hospital was enough to get her attention. On the way I reassured her by saying, "They will run a few tests and we will be back home in time for me to shower and shave and get to work." I was wrong.

It cannot be explained what made me decide to go to the hospital. It wasn't a voice per se but more of a feeling. It was as if a friend had asked me for a favor and as I said before it is always hard for me to say no. I walked into the emergency room under my own power and then flat lined in the lobby in front of my wife. Had I gone to work or even stayed at home this story would have quickly ceased with the words, "The End," but it didn't. I had a 98% blockage in my left anterior descending artery. It is what doctors informally call the widow maker. After surgery and two stents I was told the recovery period would be eight to ten weeks, yet I was back to work and on the air in 30 days.

Doctors no longer call them heart attacks by the way. Nowadays they refer to them as, "cardiac events." The English language is always changing with those who wish to soften the blow of reality by coining new terms for bad things. Cardiac event sounds like a party with pointy hats and paper noise makers which unroll when you blow on them. It almost sounds fun but believe me it was no such event. One usually plans for an event or even perhaps gets an invitation I got nothing! There was no prior notice of any kind and being one who has thrown some rather awesome parties or events in my day I consider the term cardiac event just an admittance of very bad party etiquette and planning. "Hey, we're thinking of throwing an event and would love to have you in attendance."

"Really, when is it? I am a busy person and need to check my schedule."

"Well, it is right about now, and you really don't have a choice. So, clear your calendar for the next few months and welcome to the party! Surprise!" I am a simple man and tend to call things as I see them, and I still think heart attack or cardiac mugging is the correct term.

It should have been a wakeup call but instead it became another challenge to be overcome. I had to get back to work. My generation was taught much like my father was in his day that providing for those you care about is the measure of your love and doing so was how you received love in return. I know, it is a little warped or maybe even skewed but we all tend to repeat what psychologist refer to as the "sins of our fathers."

Not that I ever thought my father had ever sinned, but I remembered the pain of missed little league games and birthday dinners while at the same time being reminded, he was working hard to provide for five kids. As an adult I more than understand. It is better to remember those times when simple pleasures occupied the clock like throwing the baseball in the back yard or sanding a pipe organ in the garage or early morning walks in the dark when learning to deliver papers. I guess all any of us can hope for is those around us to understand our deepest motivations and judge us less for not fully understanding their own desires of our time.

When blessed to have achieved a standard of living which far surpasses any prior expectations one must ask themselves why. I am not arrogant enough to think even with hard work it is all deserved. After surviving a heart attack, the question of why becomes even larger and weighs heavily on your mind. My mind works in pictures much more so than words and even in a profession which pays me for what I say each day, I still tend to think in emotions or images. And then I simply hope the words which come out of my mouth create the same thoughts to those who might read or hear them. May I give you an example of imagery and the way in which my brain thinks?

Let's look at blessings for a moment. I have often wondered why some have so much and others have so little. I grew up in a generation which was taught by loving parents that the harder you work the luckier you get. I don't negate that at all, but life is not always fair and there will always be those who have something we desire which we do not possess. God has always been very instrumental in keeping my ego in check. There is a big difference between ego and confidence. I learned that lesson very quickly while standing on a street corner of Santa Monica Blvd and N Highland Ave. Santa Monica Boulevard is a major west-east thoroughfare running through Los Angeles County and runs from Ocean Avenue in Santa Monica near the Pacific Ocean to Sunset Boulevard. At the corner is a coffee and doughnut shop owned by actor Danny Trejo and I had stopped in to get a cup of coffee. My home is near Philadelphia, but I had been in L.A. shooting a successful show at Jay Leno's garage. I stood in the California sunshine taking my first sip when a very pretty woman across the street yelled and waved.

Being recognized always surprises me for some reason even after working on television for so long. When I say she waved I mean she did so with both arms high above her head while making a sound usually reserved for meeting people much more interesting than myself. Under normal circumstances it is usually much more sedate and happens at either the local grocery store or at the gas station when I am in work boots and farm-stained jeans and pumping my own gas. Sometimes it is at our local watering hole where my wife and I have a steady Friday night date for dinner and catching up after another busy week. Either way it tends to work itself out like a well scripted play where the dialogue has been prewritten yet not rehearsed. I will notice a woman who seems to be eyeing me up trying to put a name to a somewhat familiar face. You get a sixth sense when someone is watching you. She then walks over hesitantly with a true question mark attached to her comment and will say, "Excuse me, ...Are you, Dan Hughes?"

"Why yes. Yes, I am." And then she goes on to show me every piece of jewelry she has ever purchased from QVC over the years. We will chat for a few minutes, and I will thank her for her support and hopefully each party walks away feeling good about the time together. Stereotypes are never good but more often than not the woman is near my age or older and very seldom a Hollywood starlet want-to-be from across the street.

I looked her way then pointed at myself and she pointed in my direction. It felt good. I slowly raised my palm without waving in recognition of her recognition. Just then a man coming from around the corner accidentally bumped into me as he went to enter the coffee shop. He looked up and apologized and then stepped inside. The girl across the street looked absolutely infatuated while hopping up and down. I don't blame her; my wife would have done the same thing. The man was George Clooney and I started to laugh. When I told my wife the story she asked if I got a picture. "Of the girl?" I asked. "NO, you big dummy, George Clooney!" I told my wife how surprised I was that he was much shorter in stature than I had expected, and his hair piece was obvious even from a distance. Both were clearly lies, but she was starting to get the same starry look in her eyes as the woman across the street.

I imagine in heaven there must be a huge and ancient leather-bound book which smells of dust and antiquity. Its cover is ornately carved with intricate tooling the likes of which no human hands could ever craft. Inside is a list of each of our names and beside each one is the measure of the blessings gifted to each individual by God. I have always been extremely thankful for those which were granted to me even if George Clooney's list is exponentially much longer than my own. Okay, so life is not fair but enough good deeds and kindness towards others might just be enough to tip the scales. Now, the way I see it God is very busy. He is managing and mentoring a truly global corporation and therefore must delegate those tasks he simply does not have time for to those with lesser knowledge. Picture a middle management angel who has become bored with the repetition of daily paperwork and blessings allocation. You can't blame the guy. Day after day in eternity staring at the same pages making sure allocations go to the correct recipient with countless rubber stampings and check marks. On the day we are born certain cards have already been dealt but it doesn't mean your fate is predetermined, for I believe God lets each of us create our pathway and destiny. The early speech impediment and the dyslexia were just the cards chosen to be dealt. The blessings which counterbalanced them were loving parents who refused to allow me to think I was less than what they thought I could become. I hope I have made them proud.

Thankful as I am, my natural curiosity makes me wonder how all things come to pass. It is as if somewhere along the way two pages of that dusty old book became stuck together and the life I get to lead is not really my own. Even though I work hard I cannot help but think someone else more deserving than myself should be living on this farm with a few hot rods in the garage and a wife I know is better than me. There is a large rock on the southern corner of the property which sits high on a hill and overlooks the farm. When time allows, I sit there and wonder how I arrived at this point. Wondering if when those two pages got stuck together some poor fella in Kenosha, Wisconsin was somehow cheated out of his dreams, and I got them by mistake. I am sure the middle management angel who made the error must have caught it years ago, but no one likes to admit their shortcomings to the boss. Especially when the boss is, well THE boss. So, they let it slide and kept the oversight to themselves and all I can hope for is it buys me enough time to live in such a way that it all evens out and I am found worthy.

After ten years of lavish Christmas parties and lighting displays my wife pulled the plug so to speak and recommended a simple dinner party among close friends instead of a large celebration. As much as I embrace the holidays I couldn't disagree. Having a hundred people over is always taxing and the thought of two other couples coming over for dinner instead seemed like a nice change of pace in my busiest time of year. We still had lights up outside just not so many and lessening of wattage did not lessen my holiday spirit. I truly love this time of year if for no other reason than it reminds us to be the nice people, we would hope we could be all year long. With that said I also find myself as I grow older becoming less tolerant of certain things. Rudeness is one of them, prejudice and entitlement are two more. Perhaps it is the normal course of events as we age, and it is a difficult day when one looks in the mirror when shaving only to realize you are no longer young. You never hear of a grumpy young man, do you? A certain amount of grumpiness is earned through longevity when seeing how others can treat each other.

On the day of our get-together Kelly called me from her car and asked if I could run to the grocery store to pick up a few things she had forgotten. "Sure," I told her being the joyous grumpy guy I had become. Now, the wonderful little town I live in and am pleased to call my home is a steel mill town which has seen better days and I like it that way. Not that I wish hardship on anyone, but I respect the tenacity of hardworking blue-collar families who continue to strive to make things better for their families and the community around them. It is why I agreed to start doing civil service. People here are engaged and tend to look after each other without pretense. When it snows a neighbor will most always be there to help shovel you out and the unspoken dress code leans more towards denim and work shirts than to cashmere and designer labels. In my complicated life I tend to have both types of wardrobes in my closets. When I walk into the local pub no one here is impressed I just happen, by luck, to work on TV. To folks around here I am just Dan. It's the way it should be.

Twenty miles to the east is an area of Philadelphia known as, "The Main Line," which refers to the Pennsylvania Railroad train line built in the area in the 1850's. Most of the small towns and villages which sprung up along the rail line were done so by wealthy Philadelphia families who built summer homes "away from the city" intoxicated by the lure of the country air and wide-open spaces. The convenience of a modern train line made the commute from their smaller homes in Philadelphia to lavish estates for a weekend of social graces and relaxation much easier and they took every advantage in doing so while sparing no expense.

Today those mansions tend to be owned by trust fund babies and CEOs. The rail line still exists and runs from New York City to Washington D.C. and parallels Lancaster Avenue, also known as Route 30 and is the oldest paved road in the country. As in most cases of socioeconomics there are always dividing lines and while the homes to the north were grand estates those to the south were much humbler and occupied by the many servants needed to appease the Philadelphia elite at the time.

When tasked to go to the grocery store around here there is a choice in which to make. One can drive the ten or so minutes two towns over to the fancy big name chain store where customers carry their own shopping bags made of resource renewable hemp and one can find a wide selection of brie cheeses and scones or the local market where I know the cashiers by name. I prefer the local market. I'm not a fan of self-checkout with machines and buttons instead of just saying hello and paying in cash. I am also not too keen on having to take a paper number when ordering meat when I can simply look around and remember who was here before me. There is now talk of the big chain installing iPads on steel poles where you place your order and give your cell phone number and are texted when your order is ready. Really? After a pandemic someone thought it was a good idea to circumnavigate usual conversation for another device everyone needs to touch. It always seemed a bit easier and a lot more friendly to simply say hello to Jamir behind the butcher counter and if he was busy, he would say, "I will be with you in a moment, Dan." I don't know, maybe I am getting old and grumpier but the more hi-tech we become the less we seem to actually interact with neighbors and friends.

I pulled into the parking lot, and I guess I don't have to tell you which market it was. While doing so I noticed a station wagon loaded with what appeared to be the sum total of an individual's possessions piled high in the back windows. Now some people might say men are not very observant, but it is not true. I immediately recognized the car as a 1969 Oldsmobile

Vista Cruiser. The same make and model featured in the hit TV program "That 70's Show." I only mention yet another de-railed sideline of thought because the show chronicled my age group and I remember a friend whose mom owned one. The show was based in 1976 when I had just turned 16 and I distinctly remember us cruising the Dairy Queen parking lot on Friday nights hoping to meet girls. We never had any success by the way, but that is not important to the story. Few younger people today would even know what you mean if you used the term station wagon but those of us old enough will never forget. Anyway. I also noticed that sitting beside the car was a gray-haired woman wrapped in a winter coat and sitting in a lawn chair. Next to her was a puppy on a leash.

Now I said I was grumpy. I never said I was heartless. Seeing her sitting there in the cold touched my heart. Seeing her there with a puppy slayed me. When I walked into the store, I asked Margie who was at register two, (there are only two registers,) what the story was on the woman in the parking lot. She told me she did not know, and the woman had just shown up the night before and had been there ever since. I am sure if she had pulled into the grocery store farther to the east the authorities would have been called immediately. For someone like her to be hanging around is bad for business and worse for image. For many who were fortunate enough to be born into money they count it as a sign they are better than others and thinking anything less would mean admitting it was luck and never divine intervention. In this town we don't judge people by their wallet size, plus she was not bothering or hurting anyone and besides it was Christmas time.

I did my shopping of three or four items on my to-do list and as I did, I could not get the woman and her dog out of my mind. So, before hitting the register I strolled down the dog food aisle and grabbed a small bag of dog food and went to check out. Margie scanned my two cans of Ocean Spray cranberry sauce along with the frozen package of Birds Eye frozen corn and when she got to the dog food she smiled and looked out the window towards the parking lot. Now, a local grocery store clerk knows more about you than your barber or your local bartender ever will. The bartender knows your intimate gripes and complaints; but Margie knows if you have hemorrhoids by the Preparation H ointment cream you tried to slip by her between the bunch of bananas and the Cheerios on the conveyor belt. She knows we don't buy store-bought brand-named kibble for our dogs. Hey, I am on TV remember, we can afford the good stuff. She raised an eyebrow and looked towards the window once again. "Just put it in the bag." I told her.

Walking back to my truck I put my items on the front seat and walked over to the woman hoping I would not offend and said, "I saw you here and I don't wish to overstep my bounds, but if it is okay, I would like to give you this and Merry Christmas." I handed her the dog food and reached into my pocket and handed her a $20 bill. The woman looked up without saying thank you while taking the money and then said, "Yah know, a nice lady earlier gave me a *big* bag of dog food and $100 bucks."

Well, hello again grumpy old man. Her comment caught me so off guard I found myself in the unusual situation of being at a loss for words. I might have mumbled, "Well again, ... Merry Christmas," before walking back to my truck while grumbling to myself. It was not the proper place or time to have said anything else. When you have grown up in the Midwest like I have, you do not voice your dissatisfaction with others in public, you just talk to yourself on the way home as all good people should do. I was raised in a world of please and thank you. Not just in terms of generosity but in everyday situations; "Please pass the mashed potatoes," and, "thank you very much." Our mashed potatoes were most always instant and came out of a box from either Betty Crocker or some guy named Hungry Jack unless it was a special occasion or a birthday dinner, but one always remembers to be polite. The woman's reaction was so unexpected it put me in a snit.

I did not know the woman. Nor did I know her full circumstances and all of which had brought her to be sitting there that day in a lawn chair next to a station wagon in a parking lot at Christmas time. On the drive home none of those factors were on my mind. There was a long conversation between me and me, which now while looking back, I am not proud of. I try my best to be a good person, but I guess we all sometimes need a good reminder of what that truly means. My funk stayed with me the rest of the day and festered long enough for my wife to notice it with good friends at our dinner table. Our house was lit with Christmas lights. The table set with our best china. The meal although not extravagant was warm and filling and yet I could not get that woman's reaction out of my mind.

My wife called me out, "What's your problem," she asked without any harshness.

"I'll tell you what my problem is (the grumpy man said), you asked me to go to the grocery store and I did. For the sake of time, I went to the local market. When I pulled into the parking lot there was a lady there, with a station wagon!"

"Yeah, I saw that earlier," my lovely wife said, "Did you see she had a puppy?"

"Ohh, Yesss. Yes, I did." I said letting as many syllables hang in the air as long as possible…. With her simple question of few words, I closed my eyes and lowered my head. Our town has 13,000 residents but I know my wife.

"I felt so bad for her," my wife started to say.

"Let me guess," I told her, "You gave her a big bag of dog food and $100, right?"

"How did you know that?" my wife asked, truly amazed.

I started to chuckle and then the chuckle multiplied to a laugh which the more I tried to stifle the more it demanded to come forth. The sound was more like a series of staccato wheezes which escalated until tears rolled from my eyes and both couples and my wife looked across the table thinking I might have had a break down. When I could finally take a breath I said, "You out-niced me! You did it again. How is it that you always seem to do that?" I asked. "Even when I think I am at my best you somehow seem to be able to do that." I told them about my small bag of dog food and twenty bucks and told them of the woman's reaction. The coincidence was funny but knowing my wife it was not a coincidence at all. I embellished it for comedy effect. The impersonation I did of the old woman was now with a British accent as if having been offput by missing the Queen's tea. Feel free to do your own British accent while reading the next line… "A much nicer woman than yourself bestowed upon me a much larger bag of dog food and …a hundred dollars," and we laughed. Please, tell me you played along and did the British accent. I don't want it to be one of those you had to be there moments.

One of our dinner guests commented it was still rude, but I no longer agreed and was about to say so when my wife beat me to it as usual. She asked, "Is that why you were so quiet today?" I sheepishly nodded. "Isn't kindness supposed to be its own reward?" Ouch. She was right. She always is, and twice in one day I was out-niced but wiser because of it. I'm finding the older someone becomes the more they become themselves. Whether it be grumpy or otherwise. It doesn't have to be that way though. I just needed to be reminded. It was one of those times when you see the obvious for the first time and chastise yourself for not having seen it earlier. I was still chuckling to myself when the conversation turned to other topics and my wife patted my knee under the table with a smile.

In hindsight, the woman I do not know, had received *two* bags of dog food and $120 bucks. In doing so I had thought I had been slighted of a thank you I thought I had deserved. In the moment I realized the thank you didn't matter at all. In fact, it was my own sense of manners which are supposed to be actions of grace which were actually the cause of my own anger. I judged someone thinking they had not lived up to my own standards when I could not imagine sitting in a cold parking lot and homeless. I excused myself from the table for a moment and stepped outside the front door and onto the patio. Leaving the warmth of our home with friends gathered at a table and Christmas lights made the cold of the outside feel even colder. Not as cold though as I imagined it must feel to that stranger and I thought of her and thanked her for her gift to me in remembering what was important. I bowed my head in a bit of shame and stood there long enough to make sure I felt the chill and stepped back inside. When I got back to the table, I asked those who were present if they wouldn't mind saying a prayer for the old woman and her dog, and we did.

My wife, who will always be nicer than me, sweeter and more giving than I can ever attempt, reminded me of the simplest and most important message of the Christmas holidays. She also had a little help from a stranger. To give, expecting something in return is not true giving. When one gives with no expectation of anything in return, you truly embody the spirit of what Christmas is all about. The fact the woman might still think to this day I am a cheapskate doesn't matter. She received the gifts and I hope in my earlier grumpiness they helped and made a difference.

I purposefully drove by the grocery store the next morning, but the Vista Cruiser was gone along with its occupants. I sat there for a moment or two hoping she had made enough to get back home and wished for her that there was a home in which to return to and someone waiting who might have missed her. It saddened me to think anything otherwise, but I will never know.

I think back to the woman and the story each year and each time it makes me smile. Thinking of how I was out-niced and how hard we all laughed when the reason became obvious. I still wonder what might have become of the old woman and it forces me to think outside myself and count my own blessings. The lone woman and her puppy will never know it, but I would have liked to have thanked them. We all tend to find what we seek and often it takes someone to remind us of what to be looking for. Especially at this time of year. In many cases it is a stranger who does so without effort or intent of teaching. A woman whose name I will never know taught me to look for the good in people once again without judgment or ego. My wife taught me the important lesson that generosity is not a competition. Some competitions can never be won but putting yourself willingly into the game is always more important than just watching from the sidelines.

I truly wish you and yours the very spirit of the holidays.

There are no reindeer or Santa Claus in this particular story. Sorry. I will save those for the last one I wish to tell. The one I remember the most.

Chapter 14

Reindeer Poop, Wonder Bread Bags, and Rubber Boots

Christmas comes with its share of dilemmas and catch-22's once you become an adult and have children of your own. The mindset of a child is much different than that of a parent and I have been both. My length of term as a child was perhaps longer than most with my developmental issues but the lessons my parents tried to teach me were based on preparation for the long run. Most child psychologists say children start having doubts about our old friend St. Nick around the age of eight, yet I held on to my own beliefs a bit longer. A psychologist and professor from the University of Exeter, UK, by the name of Chris Boyle posed a survey question to the world in December of 2017. It was the very first international study dedicated to what children thought when they first found out, that Santa wasn't... well, you know. He was curious as to whether the belief system varied by country, between religions and by religious affiliation. Boyle asked adults when they no longer believed and how they found out. He also wanted to know if Christmas was different after that.

A third of those who took the time to respond to the survey admitted to having felt upset when hearing the news when finding out Christmas was not all they had thought it to be. Fifteen percent said they felt somewhat betrayed by their parents while ten percent wrote that they were angry. Almost a third said it effected their trust issues with their parents. It is a difficult predicament for parents when hoping to shelter their child from the cruelty of life's realities for just as long as possible. As a father I spent many a Christmas looking through the eyes of my daughter when she was young. Hoping to hold onto time. I will probably always ask myself if it was for her or for myself. There are few parental joys which can compare to the look of joy and magic on your own child's face during the holidays. Wouldn't it be nice if that could last forever?

As trusting as young children might be very few are stupid. That one word, stupid, is still a trigger for me even to this day. The word is not allowed in my house on any occasion or for any reason when commenting on another human being. I find daylight savings time to be stupid, but you will never hear me refer to another person as such. As a child I never believed in either the Easter Bunny or the Tooth Fairy. I have witnessed toddlers at Disney World burst into tears and recoil in fear when approached by Mickey Mouse and I don't blame them. Parents sometimes forget a child's perception of what is real and what is not is based purely on their observations in the moment. We also tend to forget the mixed messages we send our kids. We tell our children not to talk to strangers, yet I have seen parents push and coax their kids forward to say hi to Mickey as if he is a friend. We ignore the fact that just because *we* grew up with Mickey as an ambassador of all things magical in a kingdom of pure fantasy it doesn't mean our children have the same realization when confronted by a six-foot tall rodent in a tuxedo coming towards them with outstretched arms. Most inquisitive toddlers can also spot a cheap costume store bunny at the mall during Easter and even as a kid I questioned the rationale of a fairy who collects the teeth of small children and is willing to pay for them as well. As an adult I have no clue as to why we still perpetuate the story. It's a little creepy. I am not up to date on the legal statutes, but I am pretty sure the buying and or selling of body parts from toddlers is somehow illegal in most jurisdictions, is it not? The tooth fairy sounds like someone whose name should be on a criminal watch list and under twenty-four-hour surveillance. Right?

Santa was always different. We always welcomed him into our home with a plate of cookies and a glass of milk. We thanked him for coming and the cookies and milk were as much a bribe in hopes he would once again return next year. From the day I figured out shopping mall Santas were imposters it did not diminish my love for the guy. I remember my mother asking me if I could keep it a secret for it was not my place to ruin it for anyone else's holiday by being a showoff. "No one likes a know-it-all, Danny." Know-it-all. Wow. I had never been told I was someone who knew it all. I kept the secret and never told anyone. (Well, until today.)

Being a parent is a lot of responsibility when knowing your child looks up to you for wisdom. They expect us to know it all even when we know we don't. They expect us to do right. They look up at you with innocent eyes while still believing in you more than anything else. Then Christmas rolls around. So, what do you tell them and when?

Children are supposed to look at the world only through their own eyes. It is not upon them to consider all their parents contend with on a daily basis and it is cruel of us as adults to share such burdens. Most of adult life is a dichotomy of sorts especially when raising children. We hope to instill confidence and teach the virtue of honesty yet at the same time we stretch the truth. Often it is with those best of intentions we wind up telling the biggest lies. Participation trophies come to mind as an example.

There were no participation trophies when I was growing up and although I understand wanting to teach our children, they are special and significant do such things also paint an inaccurate picture of what our kids will face in the future? I wanted and even dreamed of being a professional baseball player when I was eight. It is why my father gave me the baseball signed by Roberto Clemente, but the fact of the matter was I sucked at baseball. I was way shorter than everyone in my age group and with ADHD I had the attention span of a gnat. Would participation trophies have just encouraged one who has always been a dreamer to pursue a future in an endeavor with reasonable limited outcomes? Would I have become embittered and unproductive thinking the world had wronged me, when my participation trophies told me I was equal to everyone else? Probably.

Often times when wishing the best for our kids we simply forget what being a kid is all about. On a rare occasion when

Dad was not working, he was able to attend one of my games. Four inches shorter than most kids on my team I batted leadoff for the last third of the season. That's right, first. Any coach worth his salt knows to put his best hitter up first. He's the one who can hit the ball consistently and increase the probability of a base runner and therefore a potential run. Most are good at making contact on a regular basis and are strong athletes. The strange thing is I was neither. This is not a bad parable in which to compare adults to children.

Adults think in terms of score cards. Competition. Beating the opponent and adding up the tally at the end of the game to declare yourself the winner. Who did you beat and who did you best and who were you better than. At batting practice for the first two thirds of the season and in every game, I never hit a fair ball. Not once. There were occasional foul balls and tip offs purely by luck but every other single time I swung the bat, I missed. There are nine players on a baseball team. My appropriate place on the batting roster had been last and I struck out a lot. It was frustrating but I didn't care. I just enjoyed the game. I swung at everything and missed. Low and outside, high and wide; the pitcher could have thrown the ball over the backstop, and I still would have swung. Because that's what I thought baseball players did. Pitchers throw the ball and batters swing at it. I had no thought process of the mechanics of the game yet and any concept of patience was far into my future. It didn't matter. I was playing baseball. My coach noticed something and pulled me aside and told me from now on never to swing the bat! Rest it on your shoulder! Being so short and the way I crouched at the plate he realized something no one else had ever observed. I was so short and when bent over few pitchers in our baseball league could put a strike over the plate between my shoulders and my knees. Umpires call it the "strike zone." My batting average afterwards was still 0.00 but my on-base average for being walked with four pitches outside the strike zone became .640 so I started first.

It infuriated other coaches as if our team had cheated, but it got me in the game instead of three strikes and you're out and headed back to the dugout with my head held low. Both baseball and life have rules. True winners don't ignore the rules or break them, they simply look for ways to circumnavigate them to their best advantages and still stay within the boundaries set by others. I was an easy man on base for the coach and another opportunity to add to the score card.

Baserunning was my favorite part of the game and was a pretty good heads-up player when on the base paths. Base runners score runs and influence the outcome of games and I enjoyed crossing the plate. Especially when it won us a game and teammates patted my back. I didn't care how I got on base and neither did the final score card. Looking back comes with the realization of having lived most of my life with the same attitude.

I do not remember the score of a single game in little league. Most cases I couldn't tell you if we won or lost because as important as it was to the coach and many parents in the stands, it was not what I was focused on. The first game my father was at was one hard to forget though. It was close to the end of the season and with his work schedule the first he was able to attend. I think he did so after a conversation with Mom saying I wished he could be there to see me play. The next game he was in the stands with my mom. The count was 3 and 0.

Three balls no strikes. One more ball and I got to run to first base. It was late in the game with one out with runners on first and second. I was good at running and fast too. The pitcher slowed his roll and lobbed one over the plate just hoping to get a strike. The thought of walking a third base runner and loading up the bases is daunting to a pitcher knowing there are stronger hitters coming up later in the lineup. Plus, the short kid never swung.

The distance from the pitcher's mound to home plate in little league is 46 feet. It's not much. But within that distance and with my father in the stands I made a decision. The ball looked like a ripe grapefruit, and I took the bat off my shoulder and swung as hard as I could! I heard but did not see the "tink" of an aluminum bat meeting its mark knowing I had made solid contact and saw the ball sail just over the head of the shortstop. I had never had a base hit in a game before. It was a first for me. A base hit! The sound of cheers came not only from the stands but also from my team's dugout. In the confusion of new experiences, I paused long enough to look towards my father. I wanted to know he had seen me. My father was on his feet in the stands applauding, and it was him who pulled me back into the moment by waving his arm and yelling, "RUN."

I had forgotten that part. Can't blame it on dyslexia because I had run to first base plenty of times before after being walked, but never after hitting the ball. I dropped the bat and ran as hard as I could in the direction my father was circling his arm in...straight towards third. Much to the surprise of anyone watching and especially to my teammate who had been on second but met me at third base shortly after I had arrived. He turned to head back towards second only to see that base occupied as well so he froze as the center fielder scooped up my slow roller and threw it to the short stop who tagged him out and then threw it to first base where I should have been standing for a double play and the end of the inning. In hindsight I remember hearing laughter, but it didn't matter. I had hit the ball.

My father asked me on the way home why I enjoyed baseball so much. Perhaps in his adult mind he too was thinking of score cards and wins and losses. Whereas many parents nowadays tell their children unrealistically they can be anything they want to be, my dad was more of a realist. "You know Danny most of the kids on your team are bigger and stronger than you. The chances of you ever playing pro ball are slim to none."

"Frank, he's eight!"

"Well better off hearing of it now instead of getting his hopes up." He asked again why I love baseball? "I get to hang out with my friends and baseball is fun. I hit the ball dad; did you see it?"

"Yeah, son I did. Hell of a hit." My mother who hated profanity chastised my father, but my father just smiled at me in the rear-view mirror as he drove home and said to her, "It was! Right over the infield." My father didn't crush my dreams with his comment. He was right and yet he took my answer as personal truth. He told me baseball was only a game and as long as it was something I was passionate about then nothing else really mattered. I still love baseball and continued to play for the simple joy of the game. I played all the way through my sophomore year of high school until the reality of reality was obvious. I even lettered in my freshman and sophomore years after working hard on the fundamentals and became a darn good second baseman with a quick glove and a much better batting average. When Dad told me I would never go pro I simply took his word as gospel and did what most children do; I simply switched my dream to being an astronaut instead.

Children are supposed to dream and fantasize. It's how the part of the brain which fosters creativity and original thought are spawned. They are not supposed to feel the pressure of life changing decisions at an early age. Let them be children. I am sure there are true exceptions to the rule, but I wonder how many eight-year-old violin prodigies actually hate the violin? Parents want the best for their children yet these days I often see those who demand their children *be* the best. There is a difference. Life is like baseball in many ways and there are important lessons to be learned even if you're not the superstar. You don't always have to be the hero to know you have contributed to the team. Just enjoy the game.

Wait, wasn't this book supposed to be about Christmas? My bad. I think real authors refer to it as going off on a tangent. In my head it is just the way I think. Always starting out with a simple story in mind, and then often times finding myself out somewhere in the weeds wondering how the pathway led me there. Thank you for reading this far and more so for your attention span. This time I will try to keep it on track.

So, let's go back to the original question. As parents how much should we coddle our children and for how long? The dilemma is this: is honesty truly the best policy at the holidays?

We all know how fleeting the first few years of a child's life are when they trust everything told to them by one who is older and thought to be wiser. They look up at you with pure innocence in their eyes excited about Christmas and it just seems cruel to ruin the mood. So, we let them dream for just a bit longer and harbor them from the adult world which we have all come to know as often fraught with disappointment. The most interesting of statistics from Professor Boyle's study was more than one third of adults surveyed said they wished they still believed in Santa to this day. I guess it is why few people ever refer to our current timeline as, "the good new days." Christmas is a feeling as much as anything else, and again I say so in terms of secular celebrations and not those surrounding religious or sectarian beliefs. It is the one time of year we allow ourselves to look at the world through the eyes of our inner child which hopefully remains in all of us. A time when dreaming was par for the course and humanity looks as we would hope it to be and nothing less.

I continued those Christmas traditions instilled in me as a child once I became an adult and a parent. The snowy boot marks made of powdered sugar and a scant hint of silver glitter left on the living room floor for my daughter for her amusement were mine and not Santa's. Guilty your Honor. (After trial and error, I found powdered sugar looked more like snow than baking flour.) In Boyle's research he found out something he thought fascinating although I already knew it many years before and without a PhD. Most children admitted to coming to their final decision on Santa's true identity by observing small errors committed by the perpetrators of the story or by piecing together reasonable doubt in the story itself. It wasn't classmates or older siblings who convinced them. Children don't stop believing in Santa just because of age ….

The first mistake is assuming there are limits to a child's level of inquisitiveness when they think something is up. Five to eight-year-olds are like grizzled criminal investigators when curious and can fire off the question, "Why," so many times and at such a rapid-fire rate even the most hardened criminal or fibber cracks under the interrogation. They know they have you under the hot lights and just keep asking the same question until they sweat you out or until you make mistakes.

We self-appointed keepers of Christmas miracles must remain steadfast and always be prepared.

Rule number one: Never leave a price tag or store sticker on a gift supposedly from Santa. It is an amateur move and sure to get you busted. So, never underestimate your competition.

Number two: Never hide a present from Santa where a child can find it weeks or even months before the holiday. The "I told them not to look in the closet," strategy rarely works. It is only effective when used as a ruse or red herring when never intending to hide anything there but still hoping to throw a blood hound off the scent. Remember at Christmas time all children, even those who are the most honest, become detectives having no concern for search warrants or search and seizure laws. In their minds they already have inklings of probable cause and are now just searching for evidence to prove their hypothesis. Long before I knew what a hypothesis was or any clue as to how to spell it, I was worthy of a trench coat and a meerschaum pipe like Sherlock Holmes. Finding a present under the tree with a Santa tag on it which had already been spotted is a dead giveaway. Santa only delivers presents on Christmas Eve. Try a little harder parent. Have you forgotten what you're up against?

Rule number three: And possibly the most important. Let me ask you... Would the world's greatest counterfeiter of either cash or art use their own handwriting when signing a forgery? NO! Yet it is the easiest mistake made which separates the masters of Christmas deception from the rank amateur and my father was indeed a master craftsman in every way. Perhaps the greatest of all time. He had a rubber stamp made with Santa's signature in flowing cursive script so beautiful that in and of itself it could be classified as a work of art. The iconic Coca-Cola logo had nothing on my father's forethought of what people will come to remember and the red ink stamp pad, well that was just pure genius. (I still have both to this day and use them every year.) Children don't need an FBI handwriting analyst to confirm the signature of one of their parents. Wise up. Rookie!

My daughter was born when I was twenty-four, in many ways still a kid myself. I got married in the spring five months after my twenty-first birthday and I don't recommend it as advice to those younger than yours truly, while looking back. Few at that age are ready for such an important commitment including me. Especially one which has such long-term impacts and repercussions on the future of those who put their faith in you. It was my decision to rush the issue and perhaps my abilities at persuasion which made for part of why we got married so young. My mother was petite in stature but strong in will, yet she had always been one whose body was not as strong as her mind. The lung cancer which ate away at her body took its sweet time and when first diagnosed we were told maybe a year or perhaps a bit more, if lucky. I was fourteen almost fifteen at the time and devastated as any child could imagine. Important family issues in our home were always discussed as a family and always while sitting at the kitchen table. If my father called a "family meeting," it was always taken to be a serious need for discussion. My father called the meeting and stoically explained what the doctors had discovered and then excused himself and walked out to the garage. It was the first time at such a gathering he was not the moderator and the one in charge. My mother went on to inform us of the diagnosis and factors involved with the same voice she might have used when asking how our day at school might have been. I remember crying but also remember she did not. Her calmness and resolve forced both myself and my siblings to respond in likeness, purely out of example. She asked each one of us in turn after telling us she was going to fight it. What would each one of us like to see in her future before God made the decision to call her name, and my answer was self-centered. Overwhelmed and completely unable to think I told her I wanted her at my high school graduation.

I knew I could never have gotten as far in an education system which counted only test scores and achievement rates without her constant mentoring and going to battle for me. It was important to me she be there to see how her efforts had never failed me and to share the victory together and not alone. Her answer was, "Okay, I'll do my best, but you know I can't make any promises. Your schoolwork is going to be on you and if I am going to fight this then you have to fight equally as hard. Does that sound fair?"

We both defied the odds. Her so more than me, I guess. I buckled down on my studies and chose to drop out of baseball after my sophomore year to work on my studies. It still took two years of summer school with Mr. Fruits and English classes but looking back there are no regrets. Often times our greatest challenges also bring the greatest rewards and unexpected blessings. I received my diploma, and my mother was there to see it. My graduation class from North Central High School in Indianapolis 1979 was the largest the school had ever seen. I may be wrong on my numbers as I often am, but it was more than a thousand graduates. The ceremony was over three hours in length and held in the field house of the Indianapolis State Fair Grounds on a 90-degree day in May of that year. She sat there for the entire event while on oxygen and never complained once and then laid in bed for two weeks afterwards.

A while afterwards when having regained some strength she said to me, "Well, we got that goal out of the way. What's next?"

"Dancing with you at my wedding would be nice," I told her. "I'll see what I can do she told me." I will never know if those words were spoken out of hope more for me than for herself, but she was there on my wedding day. Frail and weak and in a wheelchair but she was there. She was tenacious and I was impetuous and perhaps the combination and connection between us lengthened her adventure and hastened the pace and timeline of mine. I will never know.

I had dated in high school and was no longer outwardly the awkward kid from years before. The high school radio station and public speaking taught me how to hone a well-crafted exterior mask of confidence and a quick wit had brought me more friends than my earlier days when I reeked of insecurity and doubt. More than forty years after graduation I still have close friends from that era, and they will be with me as such for my lifetime.

Disco was big in 1979 and when I saw a want ad for a disc jockey position in the same paper I used to deliver, at a local under twenty-one-night club I applied and won the job. On my first night working there I knew I had met the woman I would marry one day. She was smart and funny and had one particular quality which stood out as not only refreshing but also unique. She had zero tolerance for deception of any kind. She would have made a fabulous psychologist but instead completed her education after we were married as an electrical engineer. When hoping to hide your deficiencies or faults the easy go to is concocting a simpler answer then having to explain. When caught, she never once let me slide yet she always took the time to ask me why in hopes of better understanding me. She did so without judgment, if the answer was honest and the intent was not harmful or self-serving. No this is not another tangent just a little bit of back story so cut me some slack.

The apartment my first wife and I lived in had no fireplace and when my daughter was six and asked how Santa got in without one, I lied. First of all, what six-year-old asks that question? My biggest fear when hearing I was going to become a father was a question of genetics. After years of testing and tutors I still feared my differences would become hers as well. It turns out I had nothing to worry about. She takes much more from her mother than myself and in many ways I am thankful. She has her master's degree and is now the wonderful mother of my two amazing granddaughters. Yet on that night while looking straight in the eyes of my innocent child I told her one of Santa's elves was a locksmith. I lied. It was the best I could come up with on short notice. It was Christmas Eve and just before my daughter's bedtime. On the most special of all evenings, it seemed an awkward time to teach a six-year-old the realities of life. We had strung popcorn on thread as a family and decorated the Christmas tree. There was hot chocolate and Christmas songs on the stereo, and she went to bed with visions of sugar plums in her head, awaiting a new day and magic. (Again, I still have no idea what a sugar plum is and none of you do either. But I was equally as excited for the coming of dawn as she was. If for no other reason, then to see the look on her face.) It was the Christmas she received her first two-wheeler bike. Not from Santa though but from Mom and Dad. I had not forgotten the lessons taught by my father early on.

There were sugared boot marks every year around the Christmas tree until the year she turned thirteen. The year of our divorce. Much of which I must admit was completely my fault for still not being mature enough to live up to what are only fair expectations of one who deserves your best. My daughter has always been much smarter than I was at her age. She had outgrown the reality of traditions such as half eaten cookies left on a plate with a half drunk glass of milk much earlier than I had. Yet she never called me out on Christmas morning for them. I knew she knew. She knew I knew she knew. It turns out 65% of people who answered Professor Boyle's survey admitted to playing along even after discovering the truth. Hmm, I wonder why that is the case at Christmas time?

Why would any two parties involved in a deception allow the falsehoods to continue when both understood it to be such? Unless there was joy to be found in the deception itself. If both sides, choose equally to go along with an untruth knowing it makes the other party happy then is it really wrong? I don't think so. If one's intent is purely motivated by bringing happiness towards another person, then where is the fault?

When I was ten, I had grown wiser and more worldly and certain doubts had crept into my head. Plus, adult water cooler talk at the office has nothing on elementary school rumors during lunch break. The only time I ever got in trouble at school was when I pushed a kid when he told everyone that Santa wasn't real. Growing up is tough enough without the pressure of having to wonder if your doubts are actually what is real and what you thought to be real was just the opposite. My mother used to joke that she had six kids instead of just five. Adding my father onto the list was in many ways her greatest compliment and in many wonderful ways she was correct. As difficult as it is for children to picture wearing the shoes of an adult, I thank my father for doing what so many parents tend to lose track of as they bend to their own worries about bills and adult pressures. He never forgot what well-worn sneakers felt like as a child even though I never saw him wear them. He was a dress shoes kind of guy.

On Christmas morning of my tenth year and four years before paper routes and the beginning of adult responsibilities, my father pulled off his greatest Christmas miracle for my benefit and mine alone. After the presents had been opened and the adrenaline of youth during the holidays had been spent, we all sat in the family room having run out of conversation and thinking the festivities had once again run their due course. Weeks or even months of anticipation which in many ways are the best part of the holidays always seemed to come to a sudden climax with little left to look forward to for what always felt like forever.

Christmas comes just after the winter solstice and additional months of cold. The pressure and worries of a new school semester coming and the concerns of having made it this far asking yourself if you were up to the challenge of future tasks. We all tend to think wishfully of Christmas and New Years as somewhat of a finish line, but it is not. As an adult there will be another fiscal year ahead and last year's results count little towards future quotas and stockholder demands of future growth. I think the one thing in common which adults and children feel is that there will always be another race to be run and at least Christmas offers a temporary respite from the treadmill if even for a little while. A chance to breath, before the next.

I have often felt myself feeling melancholy late on Christmas day knowing it is over and knowing those wonderous and hopeful feelings were at their longest span of time before returning once again. I don't think I am alone in such feelings, am I?

While sitting on the couch that morning, much inside my own head, my father caught my attention by standing in the entry way to the kitchen with a small smile on his face and his gaze focused just on me. I don't know how long he had stood there but he must have waited a bit before I noticed his stare. When I looked up, he raised his eyebrows with a twinkle in his eye and motioned me with a nod of his head to follow him. Not sure why and a bit confused I did what I was told without a single word being spoken. When I got to the kitchen he whispered to me, "Go get your coat. I want to show you something."

No one noticed I had left the room except my mother. She met me and my father at the front door telling him, "He is not going out there dressed like that, it is cold outside." Good mothers from the Midwest are always quite concerned about their offspring suffering the ultimate consequences of the common cold. They always preface it with the worst-case scenario of doom and gloom and never prefaced their warnings with anything less than death. They never say he might acquire a sniffle or perhaps develop a runny nose it is always, "he'll catch his death from cold!" A sure-fire way to bring on such catastrophes in my mother's mind was wet feet. Wet feet were always a harbinger of imminent demise to a child in the Midwest during the winter and needed to be avoided at all costs. I don't ever recall losing a classmate to wet feet, but it was feared the way Polio was to the previous generation. It is why she always had an ample supply of used Wonder Bread bags sitting by the front door and is a well-known ritual to all who grew up in the 70's where I did. First you slip your feet into the Wonder Bread bags with socks on and then slide them into black rubber snow boots which were usually two sizes too big due to the mathematical equation of hand me downs and the variable of how many older siblings you had and how far apart their birthdates were. When you are the youngest, like me, you could only hope for slow and steady growth of an older brother unless you be saddled with two winters or even perhaps three of clumping around in boots much larger than your own feet due to one good summer of growth spurt on his part. I still think my brother Donald did it on purpose.

You either know what I am talking about or have no clue at all. For those who remember snow boots in the 1960's or the early 70's they were the black rubber ones, (always black, never any other color. Things didn't get fancy until the 80's.) I think they were made of recycled tractor trailer tires, and they had those confounded metal buckles no little fingers could ever flip closed or open if your fingers were anything less than room temperature. Mom always referred to them as galoshes and walking in them was almost as difficult as wearing swim fins. They were demoralizing but mom insisted. She asked my father if I might need my mittens as well, but he told her we would not be outside for long.

I found myself out in the front yard standing next to my father while wearing a winter coat, galoshes and still dressed in my pajamas. Apparently wind-chill factor has no bearing on a mother's fear of death by viral infections. It had snowed the night before on Christmas Eve which always made the holiday even more special. I always loved the purity of seeing freshly fallen snow before footprints have been left behind. Something about a landscape of uninterrupted or undisturbed white snow seems awe inspiring and fresh. The house I grew up in was much like all the rest on our block. A two-story colonial with an attached two car garage to the right with a driveway which lead to the garage door in the back. My father led me to the middle of the yard and turned facing the house, so I did the same. He stood there silently for a moment as if expecting me to say something. He looked down at me with a smile and then looked up again at the house once more. I was confused. Nudging my shoulder with his elbow I knew he was looking for a response, so I gave him one. "What?"

"You don't see it," he asked.

"See what?"

"Look again."

"At what?"

"Just look again and tell me what you see."

The snow which had fallen was barely more than a dusting but was just enough to cover the low grass. The wet snow had stuck to the bottom of my awkward boots leaving unmistakable footprints just like they did with my father's dress shoes. I was hoping he would give me a hint, but he did not. My father was the type who tended to let me figure out things for myself when he felt a lesson was to be learned. He did not seem impressed when I mentioned my footprints, so I turned my attention once more towards the house. The garage is only one story, and the roof is easily seen from the middle of our small front yard and from the street. It took me a second and I had to look twice but I saw it, or rather them. The thin veil of snow had been disrupted by two parallel lines revealing the roof shingles below. They were perfectly spaced apart by roughly four feet bisecting the square roof line into two triangles, one at the upper right and the other at the lower left. I asked myself why there would be lines on the roof until it dawned on me, they weren't lines, well they were lines, but they were more than that. They were tracks! Just like my footprints in the snow they were tracks. Left behind by someone who had been there earlier! The type of tracks perhaps left by... a sleigh.

"Look closer," my father said. Even in my wide-eyed excitement of the possibility that perhaps all my doubts had been unfounded, I still waivered. I doubted my own eyes. Those of us who tend to be emotional and prone to jumping to conclusions sometimes need to step back and better evaluate the situation before once again looking foolish. It was then my father sealed the deal. I told you he was a master of Christmas deception. As cliché as it might sound, I literally read between the lines slowly guiding my vision from one side of the roof to the other, ... and there it was. It was ... a turd!

An, unmistakable, turd! In a world of shiny glass ornaments bespeckled with glitter I had never seen anything more wonderous than that turd on the roof on that morning! Right there before me was irrefutable physical evidence every child on Earth had ever hoped to find one day. Many had searched but none had ever succeeded. When the story got out, I was sure to become a worldwide celebrity with my picture on every front page as the one who had proven to all who ever doubted that they were wrong, and I was right!

The logic was sound and even rational. No one in their right mind could have come to any other plausible explanation. A turd left behind between two sleigh tracks on a roof top and left behind on Christmas Eve meant only one thing. Reindeer poop! Case closed your honor, slam dunk, call for the press conference then drop the mic. There was no happy dance no exhilaration just a deep feeling of cleansing that all this time I had not been wrong. My silence was not what my father had expected. Me just standing there staring at the roof and nodding my head. Kids don't understand the meaning of the word profound, but they feel it in the moment when confronted with life changing information. When I looked up at my father the smile on his face had drained. It took me many years later to understand why. In an effort to make me smile on that Christmas day I think he realized unexpectedly he had crossed a line. The joy of any prank or joke is only shared when both parties fully understand it is a game. A child does not understand their participation trophy is worthless and many put them on their bedroom shelf as a memento of their greatest accomplishments.

That moment standing in the front yard was to date the greatest moment of my life. In his eyes I saw a tinge of regret for just a second and then he asked, "What is the best part of Christmas, Dan?"

"Toys," I answered.

"No, besides toys?"

Not sure what he was truly asking there was a pause he filled himself.

"Dan, Christmas is special because it is the one time of year where whatever you believe might come true. At Christmas time anything is possible do you understand?" He pointed at the roof and continued, "This moment was meant for just you and me and not to be shared with anyone else. Our secret, okay? Let's keep it between the two of us."

"But Dad...,"

"I know. You want to tell everybody, but half will never believe you. The ones who do will wonder what makes you so special and them not so much. The only thing which matters is what you believe not how many people you can prove to be wrong. If we keep it as a secret just between you and me, it means you and I are the only ones in the whole world who shared this moment. That makes it special for us. You and me together. I know you don't understand this now, but I promise you will one day. Do you trust me son?"

"Of course, I do!"

"Then promise me, man to man to keep it to ourselves."

"So, I can never tell anyone ever?"

"I didn't say that. One day you will understand when you're a bit older and then it will become a story you will love telling your own children and grandchildren when they are ready to know the truth."

"When will I know it's okay to tell the story then?"

"You'll just know. If you ever want to share it and you have to ask yourself if it is the right time, then you know it's not. Listen to your heart and it will tell you when."

And he was right.

You won't hear many holiday stories featuring Christmas turds but then again neither had I, until then.

Most of my life has been, well, unexpected. It is what I wish for you this time of year, the unexpected. A time when the innocence of our inner youth is still rewarded for believing no matter how many trips around the sun we might have taken or how old me might have become. Remembering Christmas is still special.

I thank you for reading this far. Here is to the hope you feel all that the holiday encompasses. I wish you well and I wish you joy.

The Merriest of Christmas's to you and yours.

Dan Hughes

Afterword

The story I just told you was lost to memory for almost thirty years.

Looking back in the rearview mirror almost three decades later the memory came back to me. I had not thought of it in years. Seems a little strange to have forgotten such an impactful day but we tend to remember only stories we have told before and it was one by promise I had never spoken. It was an incredible woman I had met who coaxed it out of me. She has been my wife now for over twenty years and on our first Christmas together she asked me what the holidays were like when I was a kid. So, I told her. Every story I could remember, and we talked for hours. The stories just came flooding back and each one made me smile while telling it. The last one I remembered was the one I just shared with you, and she seemed genuinely perplexed as to why my father would go to such extremes. "He stood outside in the cold to throw frozen dog poop on your garage roof?"

"Yes, yes he did."

"Why? Why would he put so much effort into trying to convince you Santa Claus was real?"

"Whoa, whoa! You're missing the point," I told her. "I already believed Santa was real. He didn't need to convince me."

"Then I don't really understand the point, at all," she told me.

"Hang around me long enough and you will."

She will always be the pragmatic and logical one in the relationship and I will always be the emotional dreamer. We balance each other well. Again, I hadn't thought of sleigh marks and reindeer poop in decades and had never once told the story to a single soul. While remembering my father's words from thirty years before, but it was time. I told her exactly how he had done it even though my father never told me, and I had never asked. I knew because it is how I would have done it myself now knowing what I know. He had climbed a ladder from the back side of the roof with a length of 2x4 in hand and most likely a tape measure in the other. Sliding the piece of wood from the top corner of the roof to the lower right made the first sleigh mark and marking four feet from the first he laid down the second in perfectly parallel lines. He then scooped up enough snow in a bucket from the back yard and carried it up the ladder to cover his own footprints. He either used a flour sifter from Mom's kitchen or a trowel to do so but like he had always taught me it was always about the details. The one thing I did not know and the most interesting was where he got the Christmas turd? We didn't have a family dog at the time. The next-door neighbors did have a Great Dane though. So, I think it is safe to assume we know the suspect. I think back, laughing, while picturing my father chiseling a frozen dog turd out of the neighbor's yard with a shovel late on Christmas Eve and wondering what would have happened if he was caught.

My wife, who was a teacher before we met had changed professions and became a professional dog trainer for television. It is how we met. QVC had hired her to train and handle their mascot dog. A beautiful Golden Retriever named Murphy. If you by chance have watched QVC over the years you may remember him, and I certainly owe that dog a lot. Had it not been for him I would not have met the love of my life. Kelly and I have never had less than three dogs in our home at any given time and as many as six at once. So, on Christmas Eve there is never a lack of physical evidence in the front yard in which to please. My last task to complete on the most important night of the year and after feeding apples to the horses and miniature donkeys and grain to our sheep is to get a shovel looking for the perfect specimen. If by chance it is snowing, then I get a ladder and a two-by-four along with some driveway salt. Salt sprinkled just inside the sleigh tracks prevents any additional snow fall from covering the lines. (My father never thought of that one, but a good student always wishes to best the best teacher who ever taught them.) Details. It's always in the details.

There has been a Christmas turd on my roof every Christmas morning since Kelly and I first said I do. It is now our tradition or at least mine and each year she walks out into our front yard with me begrudgingly, but she still smiles and hugs me. On Christmas morning she allows me to believe all the wonderful things I remember from my childhood with absolute resolution and never any protests. In my house at Christmas time Santa is real and always has been.

My two granddaughters are still young and are yet to see sleigh marks on the roof and the unmistakable proof of miracles manufactured or otherwise. They live with my daughter six hundred miles to the south, but I hope now that the pandemic has subsided, this year we will all spend Christmas together. The distance is not only measured in miles but also in time lost due to me having fractured the marriage between myself and her mother. Now that we are both adults a lot of those wounds have been healed through honest conversation. If I get the chance to stand in the front yard with my grand babies on Christmas morning, I will repeat the same words my father spoke to me and ask for the same promise from each. I will also tell them the more important words of them knowing in their own hearts when the time is right to share what they have seen. They are smarter at their age then I was and I have faith in both of them.

Although it's been said many times, many ways, Merry Christmas to you.

Dan Hughes.

P.S. Before closing this book and placing it in a bookcase to collect dust I can only hope sharing these stories touches you in a fraction of the way rethinking them has touched me. Thank you for reading this far. Take a moment and look at the cover once again. Look closely.

Acknowledgments

First and foremost, I would like to thank those of you who have followed my television career over the years and now that it is over, I thank those who have supported my dream of putting words in my head on to pages of paper in ink. Few writers ever make enough money to feed their families so to be given this opportunity is more heartfelt than my humble words can convey.

This is the usual part of a book when the author expresses their gratitude to those by name who have contributed so much. I hope I have already expressed my appreciation to them personally in quantities I pray are sufficient. Those mentioned in writing have already been thanked many times. Most people don't read the acknowledgements at all but if you have chosen to read this far allow me to mention their names. Names on paper you do not know mean much to the ones who read them but to those who wrote them they mean everything.

The book you just read was rejected by more literary agents than I can count. The rough draft sent with all its syntax errors and dyslexic spelling mistakes was enough to have been tossed in the trash before looking past the rules and judgment of the story itself. Yet, there were those few who took the time.

I have two editors. The first is Donna Clayton. She burned threw a lot of red pens while being tasked to create cohesiveness of the writings of a man with OCD and ADHD while still allowing my words to be my own. I think we make a good team. If you enjoyed this book thank her, for I could not have done it on my own.

The second is Amy Brown Thorton who proofread my final draft with an eye which can only be described as equally OCD as my own. She misses nothing. A comma here or rewording a sentence in such a way that my original draft would no longer bring me the embarrassment of my shortcomings cannot be expressed fully.

To my publisher and his team. Roger, I say thank you for believing. Not so much in me as in the story itself and the wish it might inspire others. Doing so was enough to continue hope for one who thought all too many times that his voice was not worthy of being heard.

Lastly to my father. In the span of time in which it took to put my ramblings on paper along with countless edits and rewrites, he has passed away. He was 96 and in good health up until the end. I wish he could have read them but I know him well and my adulation for him would have brought him embarrassment. Still, he deserved the admiration. This Christmas will be my first without him, but I will honor his memory once again with reindeer poop on my roof.

Other Books from the Mind of Dan Hughes

<u>Stealing the Sky</u>: Historical fiction based on facts few Americans were ever told. Action adventure. Spy novel.

During the Cold War era and the early days of 1960 America was in a space race with The Soviet Union. At stake was not only national pride, but it was also the fear of nuclear weapons pointed from outer space. Information taken from recently released CIA documents and thousands of hours poring over pages obtained through The Freedom of Information act comes the story of a Russian born female spy working with a rag tag team of NASA engineers who stole a Russian satellite from under the nose of our enemies. The story is factual. Only those characters redacted from government documents were created in which to tell the story. Historical figures were portrayed as accurately as possible giving the reader an unprecedented view from behind closed doors at The White House and 1960's politics.

Real American Publishing: Release date, October of 2023.

The Spear: Historical fiction and adventure.

Francis was born with an exceptional mind. Admitted to the University of Berlin at the age of fourteen, it was the help and support of a college professor who fully understood the challenges of attending University at such a young age which molded his formative years. The professor was Albert Einstein. In the years just prior to World War II Francis would need his wits to outsmart Nazi Leadership and even the Fuhrer himself when forced to take part in an archaeological mission he knew was not possible. Hitler was obsessed with an ancient artifact of dubious heritage and Francis had been tasked against his will to find it or else. It certainly was not the right time to have fallen in love. It is a story which spans two generations one in prewar Germany the other in America after the war. The first fought to defeat the Nazis the other fought knowing the war had never really ended.

Anger Issues: Fiction. Murder and psychological thriller.

Dr. Jamin Moore, a preeminent Philadelphia psychiatrist had become a well-known expert in the treatment of narcissistic personality disorder. Groundbreaking research had made him wealthy but when meeting his most challenging patient to date he began to question his own sanity. Sometimes groundbreaking is not enough; sometimes you need to dig a hole.

Lost Causes: Fiction. Murder and intrigue. Court room drama and a poignant look at our judicial system.

Most people think crime is what happens when bad things happen to good people. What happens when a good man loses everything and decides to turn the tables on those who are to blame.

<u>As Seen On TV:</u> Motivational and educational memoir directed towards inventors wanting to get their product on national TV. Business. Self-help. Inspirational.

Dan Hughes shares his thirty plus years of experience as a host on America's largest televised shopping channel QVC with insights on how to develop an idea and bring it to a national marketplace. In doing so the author also shares his own story of what it took for him to achieve success and happiness against the odds.

Scheduled for publication in early 2024.

Printed in the USA
CPSIA information can be obtained
at www.ICGtesting.com
LVHW022316091123
763570LV00009B/297